REPAIRERS OF THE BREACH

Repairers of The Breach

MEMOIRS OF A MISSIONARY

NAGASAKI, JAPAN

1948-1951

MARGERY L. MAYER

REPAIRERS OF THE BREACH:
MEMOIRS OF A MISSIONARY
NAGASAKI, JAPAN 1948-1951

Copyright © 2009 Margery L. Mayer
ISBN 978-1-886068-37-7
Christian Life · Religious and Inspirational · World History · WW II
Library of Congress Control Number: 2009930276

Published by Fruitbearer Publishing, L.L.C.
P.O. Box 777, Georgetown, DE 19947
(302) 856-6649 · FAX (302) 856-7742
www.fruitbearer.com · info@fruitbearer.com

Edited by Fran D. Lowe

Unless otherwise noted, Scripture is taken from *The New Revised Standard Version (NRSV)*, copyright © 1989, Division of Christian Education of the National Council of the Churches of Christ in the United States of America. Used by permission. All rights reserved.

Printed in the United States of America

Your ancient ruins shall be rebuilt;

you shall raise up the foundations of many generations;

you shall be called the repairer of the breach,

the restorer of streets to live in.

—Isaiah 58:12 (NRSV)

TABLE OF CONTENTS

PREFACE

Sixty years ago on August 31, 1948, I sailed with eight other young Americans on a freighter, the *Tradewind*, from San Francisco to Yokohama, Japan. We were part of a group of sixty young people recruited by the Board of Missions of the Methodist church into a program called the "Fellowship of Reconstruction." Fifty of us were sent into post-World War II Japan as J-3s (Japan-three years). Ten went to Korea as K-3s. We were sent to teach English in mission schools and, through that vehicle, witness to the students about our Christian faith. We wanted to break down the barriers of hate, distrust, and fear that had been built during the war between us and the young people of Japan and Korea and transform those feelings into ones of love, understanding, and respect.

Before leaving, we had been given six weeks of orientation at Riverdale Country School in Riverdale-on-Hudson, a suburb of Manhattan. Floyd and Emily Shacklock were the directors of the program.

Our four classes included "Theory and Techniques of Teaching English as a Second Language"; "Japanese (Korean) Language Study"; "Japanese (Korean) History and Culture"; and "Christian Studies." Although we knew very little about that part of the world into which we were going, we were highly motivated; and our teachers, experts in these fields, were pleasantly surprised at the high marks that we got on our exams.

I was sent to teach at Kwassui College in Nagasaki, Japan, because this was a sister school to Ohio Wesleyan University, from which I had recently graduated. The following thoughts and reflections were taken from letters to family and friends, my own diary, and events and experiences carved in my memory. As I was re-reading these, I was distressed about some of the non-inclusive language that I used back then, such as my reference to Japanese as "natives." I have left these words as they are because they reflect my way of thinking at that time.

Because 2008 was the sixtieth anniversary of that first voyage to Japan and the eighty-fifth anniversary of my voyage into this world, I have wanted to publish this collection for some time. If this book is of any interest to family and friends, I am grateful. Mostly, however, I needed to do this for myself.

Margery L. Mayer
August 23, 2008

MEMOIRS OF A MISSIONARY

September 16, 1948. Under cover of darkness, the ship finally slipped into the harbor of Yokohama, Japan. As we slowly crept forward through the channel, small lights could be seen dotting both sides of the shore. I knew that these lights shone from the homes of Japanese families—the "enemy" we had fought and killed during the four-year period of World War II.

Two long weeks before our arrival, this freight ship had slowly moved out of the San Francisco harbor. Crossing under the Golden Gate Bridge symbolized our departure from the familiar land of home and the beginning of the unknown journey ahead.

I still remember standing at the prow of the ship as we sailed into the sunset. We could see nothing around us but sea and sky. There was nothing in front of us but the sun slowly sinking into the water.

"You don't have to worry about getting seasick," my friend Peyton said in a comforting tone. "Just keep your eyes on the horizon."

I felt encouraged as I drew a blanket closer around me to protect my body from the chilling wind. My eyes were focused on the darkening horizon ahead of me. The ship sailed on as the sun set on the dark horizon.

Then . . . my stomach exploded, and for the remainder of the next two weeks I spent most of my time hanging over the rail. Wanting to protect my friends on deck from receiving the "gurgitations" of my seasick stomach, I changed sides of the ship as the winds changed.

The one event I can remember from those days, besides hanging over the rail, happened about one week out, when we were close to halfway across the seemingly endless ocean. This was the time the sailors gave us a sense of hope in the midst of the tiring hours upon hours of looking at only sky and sea and sea and sky. "Tomorrow we will cross the International Date Line," the sailors told us. "A mail boat will be tied to the line so you can mail letters home if you wish!" By this time we were not only seasick but homesick as well. We stayed up much of the night writing letters to family and lovers left in the States. We had every intention of sending these on the mail boat supposedly attached to what we actually thought was a line—the International Date Line. To believe that this was a reality suggests the small degree of sophistication we had at age twenty-five, coming out of World War II.

The sailors gave us a kinder gift as we sailed closer to the shores of Japan. They encouraged us to look through their binoculars to see if we could find Mount Fuji. At that point we felt as though we would never see land again, but with patience we were finally able to catch a glimpse of majestic Mount Fuji rising out of the clouds. From our distance, it was like a pinpoint, but it was a joyous sign that we were eventually going to step foot on land again.

What in Heaven's Name
am I Doing Here?

After seventeen grueling days at sea, we made port. We had just come through two days of a typhoon at sea that made most of us wonder if our stomachs would ever look forward to receiving food again. With this ordeal past, we looked toward the future. The ship slowly moved through the darkness, and my eyes glanced from light to light flickering dimly from houses on the shore. I realized that around the lights in those homes sat Japanese people with whom we had recently been at war—Japanese people on whom we had dropped the atomic bomb, people whose cities we had bombed. How did they feel about us as Americans? How would they receive us? How would they treat us? This journey into the unknown was about to begin a new phase. I could no longer hide under the cover of the dark of night surrounded by winds and waves, protected by the ship that carried me onward. The time had come. I would soon step onto this foreign shore and begin my life among these people.

As daybreak came, the ship eased into a docking place, and from the railing I gazed down at what seemed to me to be very little men scurrying around the dock. They spoke loudly in words that seemed to have no bearing on the introduction to the Japanese language we had struggled with during our six weeks of preparation.

But most curious to me were the feet of the dockworkers. They were wearing what I later learned were *jikatabi*, rubber shoes with a split between the big toe and the rest of the toes. "Why, Japanese people must have only two toes on their feet," I surmised from looking at these split toe-shoed feet.

The question, "What in heaven's name am I doing here?" certainly crossed my mind as I hung over that railing watching all the activity necessary to secure our ship. At that moment I remembered the letter I had received months ago from Dorothy Nyland, the youth secretary on the national staff of the Women's Division of the Board of Missions of the Methodist Church in New York City.

"I saw your brother Ron the other day, and he suggested I write to you," she had started her letter to me.

My brother Ron's version was, "As I was hurrying to my job at Macy's the other morning, Dorothy Nyland accosted me on the street. In her customary manner she opened her big, black purse, and pulling out some papers asked me if I wouldn't like to go teach in Japan. Knowing that any conversation with Dorothy is a lengthy one and not wishing to be late to work, I quickly ended the conversation by saying, 'Write to my sister Marge' and gave her your address."

In Dorothy's letter to me were two appeals. One was an appeal directly from the leaders of the Kyodan, The United Church of Christ in war-devastated Japan. It had been printed in the January 1948 issue of *Motive Magazine*, the most widely read Methodist publication for youth. The Japanese Christian leaders had written:

Send us a group of your finest young people to help in the task of reconstruction. We need them desperately, not to rebuild the rubble of our cities, for in time we can do that, but to rebuild the lives of our young people. We will place them in the most strategic places we know—in our schools and colleges where the day-to-day influence of a Christian life will count for the most. They must be effective workers; they must be willing and able to endure the hardship and deprivations of our life today. Above all, they must be people of humility and love and with a genuine religious experience they are eager to share. Send us enough of them, and in time, for the opportunity may pass.

The second appeal in Dorothy Nyland's letter to me was a challenge to join the Fellowship of Reconstruction for Japan, founded by the Board of Missions of the then Methodist Church (now the United Methodist Church) in response to the request that had come from Japanese Christians. Fifty young men and women from ages twenty-one to twenty-five—graduates from college and active church members—were being recruited to go to Japan to teach English for a three-year term. The stipend was a thousand dollars annually, with transportation, housing, and medical care provided. The Board of Missions put the challenge boldly:

> This might be the chance of your lifetime, and it might be such a tragic failure that you would never be able to forget it. It might be the most intelligent investment possible of your time and ability, and it might not be the thing for you at this time at all. Certainly, it is not a ready-made adventure, and it is not a lot of quick money. Instead, it is a stint of sacrificial service. Those who are accepted must go the whole way—the whole way in extravagant giving of time, energy, imagination, and courage. Those accepted must be capable of living in a war-ravaged country on the same level with atom-bombed people. They must be strong enough to live in rugged circumstances in compounds and school communities. They must be able to meet high standards of health, academic record, practical ability, and Christian character. But if you have

**been doing a lot of talking and have concluded that you
must do something to make your talking and thinking
concrete, then this may be your job.**

In retrospect, I realize that if Dorothy Nyland had never met my brother on the streets of New York when he was hurrying to work, and if he had not used the excuse of writing to me as a way of disengaging himself from her, I would never have heard of the J-3 program and therefore would never have gone to Japan. In 1948, I was a person of faith, but because I had been out of Ohio Wesleyan University for three years, I was not that active in a church youth group where I would have received this information directly.

How tragic it would have been for me had this letter never come to me from Dorothy. I probably would have continued in the direction my life was going at that time— toward my engagement to Bob and the traditional role of raising a family. Yet, in so many other ways my life's journey had led up to my acceptance of the challenge of joining the Fellowship of Reconstruction.

I was in college during the war years of 1941 to 1945, and I participated in the peace movement during those years. Earlier, I was an active participant in Prince of Peace speech contests during my high school days. My brother, Dick, when drafted into the Army, declared himself a conscientious objector to the war. As a soldier, he refused to bear arms and served as a medic in the Pacific Arena, including the Battle of Guam. My uncle, who preached sermons on peace during the war years, attracted peace activists to his congregation at the Methodist church in Rocky River, Ohio. On one wall of his sanctuary were stars that represented young men from the congregation who were in the service. On the other wall were stars symbolizing young men who were conscientious objectors to the war. Discussions in my home about the war were held from a pacifist viewpoint. It was not unusual, then, that when I heard about the dropping of the atomic bombs on Nagasaki and Hiroshima in August, 1945, my reaction to this news was almost violent. I strongly believed that by this act, my country, which perceived itself as a nation of Christians, had committed a sin against the Japanese people. Even beyond this, we had committed a sin against God.

It is quite understandable, therefore, that when I learned of this appeal for Christians to join the Fellowship of Reconstruction in Japan for three years, my heart responded positively and gratefully. As one grounded in the peace movement, I felt that if American soldiers were willing to give their lives killing Japanese, I should be just as willing and eager to give three years of my life toward the re-building of Japan.

I responded to the appeal without hesitation and went through the application process. It was only after my acceptance had been confirmed that I told my boyfriend Bob and my parents. Both were devastated. Bob apparently had been envisioning his future with me. My mother, a church woman dedicated to the world mission vision of the church, reluctantly discovered that her commitment did not include sending her only daughter into bombed-out Japan—a country not well known by Americans at the time of World War II. But there was no turning back, and in time Mother became very proud of me. She traveled all over Ohio, holding programs designed to enable Americans to better understand and appreciate Japan, the Christian work there, and her daughter's part of that mission.

Because of the economic devastation of Japan, our group was allowed entry only on the condition that we not become a burden on the economy of the country. We were told to take with us a three years' supply of food, clothing, and other essentials we would need for living there. Day after day, my dad and brothers built wooden boxes in the backyard that Mother and I packed with countless cans, cooking utensils, personal items, kerosene lamps, heaters, and clothes. It seemed like an endless task until the boxes were all filled, crated, and shipped to the port of departure to be secured on the freighter that would carry me across the Pacific.

On my last night at home, Dad brought the whole family out into the darkened backyard where we had worked for weeks filling boxes. The stars shone so brightly overhead. Dad pointed his finger to the Big Dipper just above us. "When you are in that strange land," he began, "look up at the Big Dipper that will shine in your sky over Japan as it does here over us in Ohio. Let the Big Dipper represent our family, and when you look at it, remember our love and prayers for you. May this give you courage and strength and comfort. We, too, will stand in the backyard here at night remembering you as we look at the Dipper and feel close to you." Dad then explained that the seven stars of the Big Dipper would represent the six members of our family, with the seventh being Buster, our dog. (All of our dogs were named Buster.)

I looked at the Big Dipper often while I was in Japan. Sixty years later, I still look at that Dipper and think of that night in 1948 when Dad led us out into the pitch-black darkness of the backyard. Of the seven stars, three are still left. Mother was the first to leave us, then my youngest brother Bob, Dad's last Buster, and finally Dad in 1998 at age 102 ¾. My two younger brothers, Richard and Ronald, and I are the remaining three of the seven.

Now, here I was, standing at the rail of the freighter *Tradewind* that had just landed in Yokohama Bay. In the midst of the crowd of strange (to me) little Japanese men, we could make out the figures of the Westerners—veteran missionaries—who had come to meet us and rescue us from this monster of a ship. I went with Mildred Anne Payne to Ai Kai Gakuen, a social center she had established.

Mildred Anne was a tall, quiet but stately, and determined missionary. I soon felt drawn to her because of her spirit. The typhoon that had rocked our ship for two days had wiped out electricity and water in many homes, a situation to which I was soon to become very accustomed.

After several days of getting registered as foreigners and moving our baggage through customs, Alice Boyer and I, who had been assigned together to Kwassui Junior College in Nagasaki, were ready to embark on the train trip that would take us to our final destination. Seeing Tokyo Station with the gaping holes in its roof and sides from American bombs, along with poorly dressed people shuffling through the streets with all shapes of heavy burdens on their backs, began to make the reality of war very real to me. We boarded the train.

The journey lasted thirty-six hours in a very crowded train. We were crammed together on wooden benches facing each other, three to a bench. We each carried our own food and water for the trip. Trash was disposed of through a hole in the middle of the train floor. The coal-burning engine of the train mercilessly belted out black dust that sought us out through the windows that had to be left open for air. Finally, we arrived at our mysterious destination, Nagasaki Station on Kyushu, the island south of the main island of Honshu, where Tokyo is located. We were tired and dirty. The train platform was crowded with students and teachers who had come to meet us.

I stepped down the steps of the train into a mass of black-haired youth all dressed in the same dark uniforms. The only thing I could think of saying was "hello." The mass of humanity let out giggles and retreated quickly down to the end of the platform away from us. Their curiosity to meet the new young American teachers was overcome by their quandary about hearing English and not knowing how to respond.

Olive Curry and Helen Moore, the two pre-war missionaries who had returned to Nagasaki some months ahead of us, warmly rescued us. Soon we were in bed in the missionary residence at Kwassui School on a hill overlooking the city. I got my first real look at Nagasaki when I awoke the next morning to a gray sky. Looking out my window through the leaves of a palm tree, I saw the black tile roofs of what seemed to be gray wooden houses in every direction and wondered then if I would ever see any color again. Everything seemed so colorless, with no paint.

First Impressions

My diary of September 25, 1948 noted these impressions:

. . . the colorlessness of unpainted buildings . . . the beauty and symmetry of the hillsides terraced for farming and so orderly . . . the use of every available inch of land to grow things . . . the large spiders, five inches across, in my room . . . people half dressed . . . men in loincloths going to the toilet in the draining ditches lining the streets . . . people, especially children, following us wherever we go . . . the contrast of the American-used buildings with those of the Japanese, i.e., the railway station in Tokyo where one side held a Waldorf Astoria lounge for American military personnel and the other side a bombed-out room for Japanese travelers . . . the special privileges for Americans, holding Japanese back to let us pass . . . putting Americans first on the crowded buses . . . people pushing and pulling heavy carts of things, or leading a mule pulling a cart . . . the bowing and bowing and bowing . . . the schoolgirls cleaning their own buildings and working in the garden around the school . . .the popular question, "How old are you?" . . . charcoal-burning buses and cars . . . women working with children tied on their backs.

Sunday, September 26, 1948:

I was surprised to discover today that the Japanese don't celebrate Sunday. The common people only have two holidays a month. How we cherish our free Saturdays and Sundays at home! On the way home from church, there were people taking up a collection in the streets for the destitute families in Sasebo—victims of the flood. And most of the schoolchildren have Helen Keller pins; the money from them goes to help blind children. These concerns for others . . . and yet these people don't have enough food and clothing for themselves. I have yet to see any very well-dressed or well-fed people.

Friday, October 1, 1948:

In chapel the YWCA girls announced that they were collecting clothes and money for flood relief—and they themselves need relief. I've not ceased to be amazed at how the people in their own need are sharing with others. Imagine my amazement to see red feathers being sold for Community Chest Week!

An early letter to American friends further describes my life and feelings at the time.

Kwassui College
Nagasaki Japan
November 7, 1948

Dear Friends:

It is Sunday, that day when perhaps more than at any other time one's thoughts turn toward home and loved ones everywhere.

This morning I put on my worst best clothes. It is Sunday, but my friends would be wearing the same scant dark clothes that they had worn to school each day. It is a long walk to the church, but the girls in my Bible class could not afford the streetcar fare, so we walked together. Only Christians observe Sunday,

and as we hurried along with the crowds on the
narrow, unpaved road through the center of town, we
were jostled by women and children bent over from
the heavy load of wood or bamboo on their backs,
or perhaps from balancing on their shoulders a long
pole with heavy baskets on either end. How often
in these past days as I have seen this familiar scene I
have thought of that phrase, "Oh, Lord, take thou the
burden from my back."

At the little church, in true Japanese style, we
slipped out of our shoes and into the room that holds
about sixty people. After my translated Bible class,
the regular church service began. I can sing the hymns,
now that I can recognize most of the characters, but I
do not understand the meaning of the words. Nor do I
understand the sermon, so while the minister talks, my
mind wanders. On the way home, one of the English
majors always tells me about the sermon.

Outside in the street is the click, click, click of
the wooden *ghetta*, the only shoes most people have.
I remembered the first time I heard the sound in the
Tokyo train station. Looking out of the window, I
saw a group of children playing with newspapers, and

the lady next to me said that they were war orphans and had no other place to go—one of the common problems in this country.

The minister is young and seems to have a pleasing way of speaking. As I looked at the simple altar, the broken plaster, and was aware of the sniffling (everyone seems to have a perpetual cold), ill-clad young people about me, across my mind flashed the picture of the well-fed, smartly dressed congregations that would be worshipping in the beautiful sanctuary of my father's church or any church in America. These people who were so young in the Christian tradition had been tested in the last war as we Americans had never been. We were worshipping together here, not in the same language, but in the same spirit and understanding.

Before the war, Ame, my friend at the organ, had been in a wealthy family of seven. All of her family and possessions were lost in the atomic bombing, and the American military government had confiscated her other beautiful home. She was moved out to live wherever she could find a place. Beside me, Kitamura, an English teacher, had been accused of being a spy because she could speak English and was a Christian. Once, she spoke about the period after the bombing when she went to the place the bomb fell to look for some of her students to dig them out and give them a decent burial. Keko, a girl my age whom I've learned to know very well, lost her father in the bombing. Her fiancé died two days after she had dug him out and brought him to her home to be cared for.

This was not a story I was reading about suffering people somewhere. These were my friends with whom I taught, played, and worshipped. Just like myself, they were young people full of dreams, hopes, and ambitions. Then, in so short a time, life was changed for them, so they had to forget about the longed-for future and concentrate on building a new life out of the ruins. They are doing it with smiles on their faces and prayers to God on their lips.

The Japan I had learned about in America was the land of the cherry blossoms and the bright kimonos. But the only beauty I have seen here is God-made—in the glorious mountains, lakes, and the glowing spirits of these people. I have seen how rich life can be, and I have often wondered if we in America with all of our fancy contraptions and social affairs have really learned the secret to a happy and contented life, at peace with ourselves and with God. The philosophy of Thoreau comes to mind: that if we would only simplify our lives how much fuller they would be. I can bear witness to the truth of that statement.

If you were to come to Kwassui you would find a school on a hill overlooking the bay; thirteen hundred students in the junior high, high school, and college; the teachers meeting for prayers each morning before the voluntary religious chapel, which is always full; the girls out early in the morning cleaning the walks, yard, and classrooms before classes; teachers and students playing together until late afternoon, since there is no other place to go; the college girls having a Sunday school teaching Bible stories with games and songs on Saturday afternoon to neighborhood children; the YW girls collecting clothes for relief for a nearby flooded area (when the clothes ration per person is two yards of goods a year, no ready-made things, and no shoes except on the black market); and the girl with three rice balls for her lunch sharing with the girl who only has one. (The food ration is small, and sometimes it would be just one thing for a whole week such as only rice or sweet potatoes.) Above all, you would find happiness about such simple things, appreciation for the humblest interest, and eagerness for new experiences.

And so, this fall, while my friends in America are going over the latest style- books to select the proper length and color for a new outfit, my friends here will be wondering how to get enough clothes together to keep warm in this cold, damp climate. While mothers at home in America are scolding their children for not using a bright enough bulb for studying, my students here will be bending over one candle in a room for two to three girls. American families will be buying vitamins to take during the winter months, but adults and babies alike here will be contracting TB—not only because they cannot keep warm, but because there is no milk for the youngsters and only a simple starch diet for all.

And as I cross the next street and see women repairing the road, straining under heavy burdens, I will think of the tender care with which the weaker sex in America is treated. I have seen some beautiful weddings in my home church, but last week our cook was married by her family to an older man she had never seen. He was a sailor who wanted children to carry on his name and a servant to look after his mother.

In college my philosophy professor used to say about Christians and non-Christians, "What difference does that difference make?" I have seen what difference it has made in this land in the lives of a people who, before this, knew nothing more than working and dying. And I see how much more of a difference it must make to give humans personalities that are their own and a way of life that will make it possible for them to find the true peace and joy that can come only through Christ, who did not promise us an easy life, but strength to bear whatever life may bring us.

Next week we are having special programs in connection with the World Week of Prayer. We remember you in America often in our prayers, as we know you will also be thinking of us. May your patience, your understanding, and your forgiveness be with the people of this land, for they are struggling out of darkness and would follow your leadership toward a truer way of life.

May the happiness and peace of the Christmas season give your hearts renewed joy in the service of our Master.

Sincerely,
Marge Mayer

GETTING ACQUAINTED

There were fun and funny times, too. I remember two amusing experiences.

On the first day Alice and I went to school, we would be introduced in chapel to the student body. Anxious to "be correct," we asked the veteran missionaries for instructions. The service would be in Japanese, and we would be sitting on the stage with the Japanese principal.

"Just listen for your name," Helen told us, "and when you hear it, stand up and bow." That seemed easy enough, so after practicing correct bowing, we confidently marched off to chapel to sit on the stage awaiting our introductions.

This was the first chapel after summer vacation. The principal, Mr. Muranaka, was welcoming the students back and encouraging them to work earnestly in the current semester. The Japanese word for "earnest" is *majime*, quite similar to the Japanese pronunciation of my name, Majimeya. Mistaking the Japanese word for earnest to be my name, each time Principal Muranaka challenged the students to be earnest (majime) in their studies and be "earnest students," I stood up and bowed as graciously as I could, to the amusement of thirteen hundred students, who all looked alike to me.

In those early post-war years, buses ran by the power of a charcoal stove and chimney on the back of them. This worked well on the level road, but Nagasaki is quite hilly. Every time the bus reached an uphill grade, all of us passengers had to get out and push it to the top of the hill, whereupon we all quickly scrambled back onto the bus for the easy ride down the hill.

I soon found ways to make friends with the Japanese students. My diary, two weeks after arrival, speaks more of playing with them than teaching them:

Friday, October 1, 1948

Played baseball with a bunch of the seniors this afternoon, and they were so sweet to say they wished they could have me alone in interpretation class. How I wish so, too. Maybe something can be done.

Saturday, October. 2, 1948

Have had the most fun today of any time since being here. Had a grand talk with both Keko and Ame and felt happy about the relationships. This afternoon played baseball with the girls, and tonight went down to M.G. (Military Government) for square dancing held for the natives (sic). Ame was playing the piano. Had a marvelous time and so impressed with the way the boys and girls were so happily having a good time. They were so graceful in their movement, had such good rhythm, and for the most part decided in their own sets what they would do. For young people coming through a tradition of separation of sexes, they certainly know how to get into things and have a marvelous time. I've never seen an American group enjoy themselves any more.

Sunday, October 3, 1948

Went to my new church today with Ame and Kit. Enjoyed it so very much . . . worldwide communion. This afternoon Keko and I climbed a mountain and saw a gorgeous view of the city and sunset. We talked a little about the bomb. She told of how the rains came for a month afterward and none of the houses had roofs on them, or windows. She told how she and her family had been cut up by the shattering glass. She said, "But we are all right now," with such a cheerful air. (These people are jewels. Where in the U.S. would you see people patiently standing in long lines waiting for a streetcar?)

Tuesday, October 19, 1948

A long time since I've written, but there have been so many thoughts in my mind. I'm still so very much impressed with these simple people in their simple lives. When the girls were being very impressed with my college yearbook, I wondered if American students with all of their social affairs and advantages are any happier than these people. Here I've really seen a life of the spirit, joy, and happiness that is real and internal, not built on temporary pleasures dependent upon earthly pleasures.

Went to the dormitory one night, and the girls were so bright eyed and had so much fun entertaining us. On the way home walking along the ridge overlooking the bay, we sang songs, and my heart was moved. We couldn't understand the words, but the companionship, the same longings, and the emotions that arose because of the music were in all of our hearts. The girls said they certainly hoped that I would come back at the end of three years.

Sunday, my Bible class hiked up one of the mountains for a picnic. The view of lakes in the valleys and row after row of peaks was just gorgeous. Kit and Ame went along, but I wished that I had not had such a cold so that I might have enjoyed it more. In the evening I went to see some Japanese dances with Keko. With my cold being much worse, I've been in bed for two days since then.

Tuesday, October 26, 1948

Had my first square dancing with the teachers. The high school teachers are always out to do things, but the college teachers seem to think a little recreation is below their dignity. Keko brought me the sweetest poem she had written in English. My, how I like that gal. I'm tutoring a high school boy for an English-speaking contest next Sunday. He is the sincerest thing, and his subject is on the importance of the mother's love in the future of Japan, if she is to be a decent country with decent people.

Tuesday, November 2, 1948

The beginning of another month. Sunday we got up at five a.m. to go hiking up Mt. Tohake with about thirteen of the girls to see the sunrise. We reached the top about fifteen minutes before the sun came up, and what a glorious experience it was, with Mogi village below, the sea, Mt. Unzen in the distance, and the sun coming up in all of its glory amidst the clouds. The surrounding mountains were glorious, too. Truly a hilltop experience. The girls burst into hymn-singing as the sight reached its climax. Then they asked me to lead them in prayer. It was a thrilling experience.

Down from the mountain in time to go to Bible class, church, and then to the English-speaking contest in the afternoon with many of the same girls. It was very interesting. Almost all of the speeches were concerned with the necessity of Japan becoming truly democratic and hanging on to its morals. It was a long day, and I was really tired. After supper, Hayashi and Shiraishi came over to talk about some of their problems and the bawling out which they had gotten from Dean Hata the preceding night. The poor gals were so upset because they felt that everything they tried to do as a student YWCA was blocked by Dean Hata. How much I enjoyed the opportunity of talking with them. They are so sincerely concerned.

On Monday afternoon, we all went to a meeting of the Christian church women of the city in a Japanese garden. We all sat around on the ground for the meeting, at which Peckie and I spoke. Afterward, we played some games, and it was really interesting to see those kimonos floating around in play. These ladies do have a sense of humor. In the evening a bunch of teachers went to M.G. for square dancing and thoroughly enjoyed it. One thing I am getting tired of is baseball. The girls ask us to play at every opportunity, and I am getting a bit bored, but . . .

Saturday, November 6, 1948

Learned that the clothes ration for these people is two yards of material a year, no ready-made clothes, and no shoes except on the black market.

Thursday, November 11, 1948

Have been having fun with my square dancing for the kids and teachers. Tonight, just before dinner, Hayashi came over to the house all excited about the worship room they had fixed up at the school and wanted me to come right over with her and see it. I don't know when I've seen anyone as thrilled as she was over such a thing. She was like a child with a new toy. How my heart ached, and how deeply I felt moved that she wanted me to come and see it the first thing. We sat alone quietly for a while and then came back. She said that her only joy is in doing things for others, and I believe it is so. She will have a great influence on the future of Japan, I'm sure. (Note: Hayashi-san did become a leader in the national YWCA.)

Tonight the music teachers had a sukiyaki dinner here for some of their married teachers. It was so much fun.

Sunday, November 14, 1948

Beginning of the World Week of Prayer. Started out with six-thirty a.m. prayer service. About a hundred of us froze on the playground. This afternoon, Hayashi-san told me that Shiraishi's illness may be very serious. Possibly the starting of TB. Makes me feel terrible to think that a fine gal like that may be in for some trouble. How I hope that nothing happens to Hayashi-san.

Last night went to Iwanaga and Kinoshita's house. More fun. Very lovely, big place. And her mother insisted that we square dance—and she in a kimono. Imagine, square dancing in a Japanese home. Seems like a funny combination to me.

Keko had a meeting all day yesterday, so we got cheated out of our usual Saturday afternoon together. How I missed it.

Thursday, November 25, 1948

Thanksgiving Day. This is my second Thanksgiving this week. The Japanese have their celebration on the 23rd, and we will have our family dinner tonight. I have not thought much about the occasion because there has been no talk about the day, but my heart is full of thankfulness for this life and opportunity that has been mine.

Last week the girls commemorated the World Week of Prayer with special services each morning before school, and on Saturday night they had their final campfire. Wood is rationed and very scarce, so the decision to burn wood for the campfire was a real problem. However, it was decided that each girl was to bring one piece, and we would have a small fire for the conclusion. About a hundred and twenty-five girls gathered on top of the hill for the occasion. It was truly a moving experience for the girls as I could tell—not from the language, but the expressions on their faces.

Some of the college girls made up a play to give to the kindergarten to illustrate the idea of world brotherhood. Girls from different nations would each sing their own song and then quarrel because each thought her song was the best. Finally, one of the other girls came in to teach them a hymn which they could all sing and be happy with.

Monday, the school had its annual picnic. We hiked for two hours up to one of the highest mountains, and there had a picnic, games, and resting for about three hours before starting down again. About twelve hundred girls went and all over the top of the mountain you could see these little groups of black tops sitting around. I was so tired after that, and although the school had a holiday the next day, I had a square dance party all afternoon. Everyone wants to square dance, and although I enjoy it, I almost wish I'd never started it.

I've been so thrilled at the way the girls are becoming more eager to speak English. I just never have a free moment. Some of the college girls come to the house and want me to come over to their classroom and talk with them. Different groups invite me to their homes, and they are really trying to speak English among themselves.

Some of them are beginning to speak of their personal problems in English. It is heartbreaking to be able to go only so far, and then the language wall is there.

At first I was concerned about coming to this land where there is so much physical need and being able to give no more than spiritual food. But I have seen that it is the spiritual food that these girls are seeking. They are searching for a faith and the good way of life, and they have to make the decision of becoming Christians without the consent of their parents. It is the spiritual life that they are most concerned about.

One of my friends asked me if I could give her an American pencil for each of the members of her little Sunday school class for a Christmas present. That will probably be a treasured thing and perhaps the only one.

In those early weeks at Kwassui, my life became strongly bonded with the Japanese college students and young teachers so close to me in age. This, after all, was one of the important reasons for our being there. The more my identity merged with the Japanese, the greater the gap I felt with the Americans—both the senior missionaries and those of the MG (Military Government) who were there to transform the basis of Japanese culture and re-train them into how to "be" and act in a democratic society.

The form the American occupation took was to send a military team to each prefecture. This team consisted of Americans who supervised the revamping of education, welfare, communications (information), medicine, public safety, and the like. The task of these Americans was to work with the Japanese heads of these departments by trying to help them improve their systems and make them democratic. Towns were organized into neighborhood blocs where the Japanese were gathered together and taught democratic ways of holding meetings and making decisions. The purpose of the Occupation Forces (the MG) was to restructure basic Japanese thought and society from the ground up to enable Japan to become a country based on democratic thought and principles. These Americans (MG) seemed sincerely interested in the Japanese as a people and truly helping them.

From my students, I learned how surprised Japanese people were by the Occupation Forces. They expected the American soldiers to be as ruthless and cruel to them as their own military forces had been to the Koreans and Filipinos they had defeated in the war. My students shared with me that the girls expected to be raped; so they cut off their hair, dressed like boys, and hid in the mountains, hoping not to be found.

Contrary to their fears, the American soldiers came in bringing food and clothing, and for the children—gum and chocolate bars. And so, everywhere I went I would be besieged by groups of children holding out their hands and calling out in their Japanese accent, "Chewing gum!" and "Chocolate!"

But, for their own convenience, the occupation forces created a lifestyle quite separate from the Japanese. In every part of the country they had their own stores (PX's) for buying American food and essentials. The better-equipped, air-conditioned cars on the trains were available only to Americans, as well as the few taxis around. The MG confiscated the better Japanese homes they wanted to live in, and the owners were forced to move out but were paid no rent for them.

A DIFFERENT UNDERSTANDING

One of the most intense discussions among the J-3s during our training period in the States involved to what extent we would identify with the occupying Americans and accept these special privileges. It was a decision we each had to make for ourselves.

Alice and I, assigned together to Kwassui College in Nagasaki, agreed that our identification would be with the Japanese people, not the American military. We would not avail ourselves of special American privileges. This included not riding on air-conditioned trains or availing ourselves of shopping privileges at the PX.

We perceived ourselves as being "in the army of Christ" and not in the army of the U.S. We wanted the Japanese to understand this, too, and see us as "different" from the Americans in the MG.

Our desire for a separate identity also soon turned our attention to the pre-war senior missionaries who had preceded us in Nagasaki.

They returned to the large missionary residence that was unharmed by the atomic bomb. It sat on a hill next to Kwassui, which was on the other side of a mountain from where the bomb was dropped.

The missionary residence was large enough to house six single missionaries—each in her own room—and two servants. The size of the house, the servants, and the lifestyle contrasted greatly with the rest of bombed-out Nagasaki and the living situation of the Japanese students and teachers. From the beginning, it was difficult for me to stomach, and my diary is rather ruthless in its criticism. Ten days after we arrived in Nagasaki, Carolyn Peckham returned to be principal of Kwassui. I recorded in my diary:

> Peckham arrived with her scads of beautiful silver and linen things of all shapes. It made me cringe to think of us living with such finery and our friends just having the barest necessities to get along with. Somehow it just doesn't seem right or very missionary. How I hated it at the station having to ride up to the school in the car, while the rest of the people who had come down to greet Peckie walked home.
>
> My disgust is extreme at what I see in the other missionaries here. Their fine linens, silverware, and talking about having servants that bow you out of the door and welcome you back in. It is so disgusting to see

this finery, when people within their very reach need such necessities. May I never become so worldly minded in such service.

In retrospect, I suppose the pre-war missionaries were living out of a different understanding—that of wanting to share the finest of American culture with the Japanese. But in post-war Nagasaki, the contrasts in lifestyles were too great, creating what seemed to Alice and me a gulf between us and our students which was unbearable. It wasn't long before we began to plan how we could move out of this house and into Japanese-style housing. Apparently this was unheard of for missionaries to do and did not fall on sympathetic ears in the Board of Missions office in New York. It would be two years before we were able to get a small Japanese house built, into which we could move.

Americans often ask how the Japanese in Nagasaki treated us in 1948. I can honestly respond that I had no unpleasant experiences. I found the Japanese, especially the youth, very disillusioned with the leadership of their country. They had been told that they were winning the war, even up to the time of their surrender. It wasn't until after the war that they began to learn about the terrible atrocities the Japanese army had committed in China and the Philippines. They felt betrayed by their country and believed that the world view which they had been taught was false. A vacuum set in, and they no longer knew in what to believe or where the truth lay. They were hungry, yes, they needed clothes, yes; but more than that, they needed a reason for struggling to stay alive.

The Japanese felt that if America had been able to conquer their country, then the Americans must have a superior spiritual power as well as military might. The Japanese youth were eager to learn about this. Studying democracy and Christianity seemed to hold out a lifeline of hope for them. We J-3s came into the vacuum. I quickly discovered, however, that I hadn't struggled enough in my own faith journey to be able to adequately share answers with them to the "depths-of-life's meaning" questions they were raising. I had to struggle to get my own faith grounded first. I had to peel off the Western cultural trappings of my faith and dig deep down to the spiritual basics that were not culturally bound. It was a long, soul-searching road that had to be traveled and would lead to either life or death.

Somehow, through my own inadequacies, some elements of the Christian faith caught on in the lives of students, as these letters I wrote home reveal:

January 16, 1949

Dear Friends:

Tonight there is a new joy in my heart. Something is happening to my girls, and therefore, to me.

These past months I've been doing a lot of playing with them, discussing my beliefs on the good life, and answering many questions about religion in a general way. I know the mills of God grind slowly, but they also grind exceedingly fine so I was not expecting any miracles to happen overnight.

The girls came back from vacation and brought something with them. When they come up to me and say with a very special light in their eyes, "Miss Mayer, I have something to tell you," I know it isn't that they have received a fraternity pin or engagement ring, but that they have found God and want to become Christians.

People here are students of philosophy and psychology, and they are facing what so many of us did in college: the desire for the scientific explanation for the necessity of religion and God. So many of them are expressing humanistic views, yet they say, "You have studied those things, and because you have and you believe, so do I." The way God works through us! I have thought again and again how many more hearts would be won to Him if only He had more helpers here on the foreign field—more witnesses to His power and love.

I have one group of girls who come back again and again with new reasons for why we do not need to believe in God. They have Communistic leanings. Yet, as I said to them, if they were perfectly satisfied with their present beliefs they would not spend so much time trying to deny God. It is perfectly obvious that they are seeking but are afraid to let go of themselves and surrender to the Master. I know that one day they will, and perhaps they know it, too. These are the experiences that make up the stuff of life. I have read about them in all of the missionary magazines, but I never thought that I would understand what it means to hear those words, "I've found God."

Sincerely,

Marge

March 8, 1949

Dear Friends:

It was her final English composition before graduation. She had not been one of the girls active in the church or Christian groups, nor in the gang of girls who especially seek our company. Her father was a scientist; and her mind was the same as his, steeped in materialistic beliefs and rejecting as pure romanticism any tendencies towards religion.

She said in this paper, however, that when she came to Kwassui she realized that some of the other girls had a certain intangible something that made life for them more than just about things and occasions. She still was not ready to accept Jesus and God entirely, but in her years here she had come to find a new happiness in a life of the Spirit and new possibilities in her own personality that she had never thought possible.

This is one girl's awakening, but I hear the same thing over and over again. I've just read a book written by Michi Kawai, one of the early Japanese Christian leaders and founder of Keisen Girls School in Tokyo. She calls this story of her life, *My Lantern*. In it she speaks of how she received her light from many different contacts, and the memories of them encouraged her to keep her lantern alight when the road was not easy.

This is graduation week. As I hear and see what the influence of this mission school has meant to these girls and how they are so anxious to spread the light to others in their lives to come, I know that the influence of our mission-giving is far greater than we can imagine. We Americans come and go; but the spirit of the schools, the Christian institutions that are mainly supported and staffed by the Christian Japanese, continue whether or not we are here. It is true that we must help these people to help themselves. For every girl we send out, perhaps we are reaching ten more through her by her contacts. It is exciting to think of the chain reaction resulting from you and your dedication to the lives of the schoolgirls here.

We must never forget that Christianity and democracy are on trial before the eyes of the world.

Cordially,

Marge

43 YEARS LATER

Forty-three years after leaving Nagasaki, I returned to visit Kwassui and friends from those days when I was a teacher there. As the train pulled into the modern station, I remembered my first arrival in 1948 and the crowd of young, black-haired, bashful students waiting on the platform to greet me at that time.

This time, in 1991, as I peered out the window of the slowing train, I saw a group of five older women waiting on the platform, eagerly peering into the windows, searching for someone they had obviously come to meet. As I emerged from the train, they quickened their steps, calling out my name and bowing again and again. They identified themselves as my students from forty-three years ago. They had heard that I was coming back to visit Kwassui, so they had traveled from their homes around the country to greet me here in Nagasaki. I had not seen them nor had any contact with them during those forty-three years.

I described this experience in an article I wrote for the December 1994 issue of *New World Outlook*:

In 1948, when I had first arrived in Nagasaki as a young American teacher, my students were about the same age as I. In Japan during the war, working in factories had replaced studying for girls; so students returning to school after the war were older. My students and I came together in Nagasaki in 1948 as youth who, in our respective countries, had been taught to hate and mistrust one another. Although we lived halfway around the world from each other, we had in our own ways experienced the horror and hopelessness of war. We were determined to find a way into a new world of peace and understanding.

The students I lived with at Kwassui were discouraged about life in post-war atom bomb-devastated Nagasaki. They had lost any sense of trust or hope in their government and what it had taught them about the purpose of their lives. They were searching for meaning and for some reason for staying alive.

I shared my Christian faith with them. We spent many hours together talking about faith and hope and love.

And so in 1991, five of my former students had come to Nagasaki from around the country because they wanted to tell me what it had meant to them in those post-war years to talk about faith, hope, and the meaning of life. They wanted me to know how important the Christian faith had been to them all through the years. With eagerness they described the various practical ways in which they were each living out their Christian faith.

"We know that missionaries don't get to see the fruits of the seeds they sow," one woman said. "We wanted you to know what your life among us meant during those crucial years of our youth."

It is gratifying to know from Christmas letters even now almost sixty years later that many Japanese students still recognize and remember the impact that those post-war years together had on their lives—rather I should say "our lives" because the direction of my own life journey was ultimately determined by the impact of those years we lived together.

REVISITING THE PAST

As I continue to reflect on those early years in Japan, I am amused and touched to find letters written during those early years about me which students and teachers sent to my parents. The first letter includes the results of an assignment to write about American teachers:

January 27, 1949

Dear Miss Mayer's Family:

Perhaps you are curious as to what I am. I will introduce myself the first thing. I am a Japanese student at Kwassui College and nineteen years old. Every day I am studying English and playing with Miss Mayer.

Sometime ago, she show us your pictures. My heart was full of much thanks when I looked at them, because I have known that she came to our school from this sweet home. Then I have begun to write this letter to you though I can't write this well.

In the first place, I should like to say thank you very much for sending your dear daughter. We all love her very much as you. I am very glad to write that she is the best and most wonderful teacher in our school. Only I am near her, I am very happy. She teaches us Christianity, English, dance and the soft-ball and she used to strike home run hits.

On Sunday, I go to church and before service I have a Bible class and hear her preach. I can't understand English very well but I can understand well her kindness and love. I want to say once more, I love her and thank you very much for sending us wonderful teacher.

One day, one of the teachers said to us, "Write a composition about American teachers." So, many of us write about Miss Mayer. Now I want to introduce some of them for you must be interested to know how we think about her.

Miss Hayashi's composition. She is president of our YWCA and my good friend:

There is no need to give you an idea of her
except to let you imagine a young deer rushing

through the forest air of the morning longing
for the sun to come up. Nobody can help her
from running and nobody can help himself from
following her.

Mine:

Her hair is short and brown. The eyes with
the brown lashes are light blue. Her mouth is red
and cheeks always pink. Her face is so fresh and
charming that we feel pleasant to see it. She is
the tallest person in our school. Her body looks
like a young and stout tree which is growing
against the high and wide skies. Round her,
there are many students always. I think that it
explains what sort of character she has. I always
know when she is coming, her low humming.
Thus, she is so active and I think sometimes
she is noisy like a little boy. But I cannot help
to think that this is one of her characteristics,
because sometimes she is so quiet and tender like
our older sister.

I can't explain what a wonderful teacher she is and
how kind she is. Can you imagine what we think about
her and how she spent her life in Japan?

It is very warm in Nagasaki but at January 16, it snows just a little and as Miss Mayer was so glad, I was glad, too.

I hear various things about your country from American teachers and want to go there really. I wait the day when I can go to see you from now. Though you live in a country beyond the wide sea, yet I am praying for your happiness and health every morning.

Affectionately,
Sonoko Ito

The following letter shows that my parents wrote to my students:

24 February, 1949

Dear Miss Mayer's father!

Thank you very much for your good letter. I have been glad very much but I am sorry that I cannot explain well with my poor English how I was glad to receive it. When I received it I could not help to jump up and cry, "A letter came from Miss Mayer's father to me!"

Miss Mayer is very well and seems so happy. Now she is wearing a red sweater and a black skirt. These suit her very much and she seems very beautiful.

Sometimes ago I went for a walk with her. It was a wonderful starry night. When we reached a seaside she said, pointing the seven stars, "They are my family" and went on in low voice, pointing each star, "That is my father, that is my mother, that is my elder brother and that is my younger brother. They must be looking up at these stars in America." I can't forget the beautiful words and I look up at your stars at every night imagining you and your family.

Sonoko Ito

The following article was written by students for the Kwassui newspaper:

The typical American whom we are associated with is Miss Mayer whose waistline is about at our heads. Don't be surprised. At first when she came here, she was walking gracefully like a Japanese girl, but now she walks two meters with a vigorous stride or leap. As our English was not practical, we were troubled to distinguish her from Miss Boyer who came at the same time; so we called them "long teacher" and "round teacher" (as Miss Boyer is so fat that she looks lazy when she walks). At a glance, Miss Mayer is charming all of the girls in college and high school, also some of the female teachers are hanging around her like kindergarten girls. Sometimes she speaks Japanese in class which she learned from the girls, but those Japanese words are very easy and we can easily understand them in English. Therefore, we feel various feelings mixed with regret and funniness. Even the male teachers are always discussing about materialism, theism, or truth to Miss Mayer, throwing out their chests, looking up at her far above. As she was brought up among brothers, she tells that she played "Tarzan" and not girls' games with them when she was a child. Her most favorite things are milk and water. So, we hope we small girls may drink milk and water to become big. We never heard of milk fat and water fat, but potato fat. We suppose she got such a stout body because she grew up in Toledo, Ohio, the productive soil of corn.

This letter was written on July 31, 1950 by the two maids who worked in the large missionary house where I lived my first two years:

I wants to tell you about Miss Mayer's daily life.
She wakes up about seven and goes to the toilet first
and is singing a Japanese children's song, *Moshi moshi*

kamiyo. Or she says, "Good morning, Morita-san. Are you happy?" After dresses up she shouts, "egg." We are excited and say, "hurry up, hurry up" and prepare the breakfast. She is very quick to eat. Other ladies finish the fruit first and then ring the bell and I bring next, but in the case of Miss Mayer, she needs not to ring. I bring boil or fried egg with toast bread at the same time. She takes all the food every morning pleasantly. We are delightful, too, but sometimes she looks gloomy, then we feel so anxious we wonder is she sick, or worry about something? We have no taste at our meal, but be at rest it is seldom she is not so well.

As the school begins at 8:00, she says in Japanese very skillfully, *"itte mairimasu."* This means "good-bye, see you later." The dinner is at twelve-thirty. She is late. Often we are waiting for her and look for her at window then hear her whistling we say, "Why are you so late?" She goes to school after dinner. The supper is at six. At dinner time she is late because she is beloved by everyone, pupils, church people and citizens. It is our joy she is loved by everyone.

Miss Mayer's Mother and Father, do not worry about her life in Japan, but we suppose sometimes she is homesick. The bath is Japanese style and she likes bath so she takes it the first time even though it is rather cold weather. There is no shower. After supper she goes by bicycle somewhere. I am lonely. She flies round like gunshot. I love her. I think so Miss Mayer go back to America next July, but she has to go home and if I think so, I must let her go back to you safely for these three years you sent your dearest daughter to far East country. You would be lonely. Please take good care and wait her back. Be at rest of herself here. We will help her with all our hearts with love. She is just like sunshine here. If it is cloudy we say she scatters the bright sunshine to over hearts passing by the street.

Of course, new experiences abounded as reflected in the following letters and excerpts from letters I wrote back to American friends:

> Kwassui College
> Nagasaki, Japan
> January 12, 1949

Dear Friends:

Winter vacation is over, and today we start the last lap of the school year. Here, the end of the year comes in March because after that the weather is too hot for the students to concentrate on exams.

Right now we would be glad for some of that hot weather. We've had our first snow, though it did not stay on the ground. The temperature in our house averages forty-three degrees, and the school is colder than that because it is made of stone and therefore damp. I suppose one of the reasons the cold seems so intense is because there is no relief from it . . . .The dampness never gets warmed out. However, one gets used to it and realizes that when no amount of clothing can keep out the shivers—well, the best thing is to forget about it.

Kwassui School stands on a hill overlooking Nagasaki Bay. The atomic bomb dropped on the other side of a mountain, so the school building was not destroyed. The force of the blast did blow out all the windows, and the roof was lifted up, coming down askew on the walls.

During the winter months, the cold winds from the sea blow mercilessly through the bombed-out windows, creating a refrigerator-like classroom atmosphere. My students—still in their summer cotton blouses and skirts, the only clothes they have—move their desks to the wall away from the windows and huddle as close together as they can trying to keep warm by the heat of body touching body. Their hands are swollen red and cracked from the cold, which is aggravated by the constant use of cold water, the only water available to them. It is almost impossible for them to hold pencils in their swollen fingers.

I stand before them to teach, wearing fur-lined boots, gloves, a winter coat, and a hat. Oh . . . the guilt I feel at what I have and they do not have. At noon, as I walk from the school to the missionary residence several buildings over, I pass students sitting on the cold ground in the sun eating lunch. Often the girl with two rice balls for her lunch shares one rice ball with the girl who has none. Girls cook their own meals in their dorm rooms over a charcoal fire in a little *hibachi*, a ceramic container something like a large flowerpot. Rice, the main staple, is rationed; and when the ration is gone, girls go down the street to buy roasted sweet potatoes for their meal.

Last week I went with one of my friends, Kazuko, to the site of the atomic bomb explosion. The only thing that saved the main part of the city from destruction is the fact that it lies on the other

side of the mountain from where the bomb fell. The
bomb exploded in air, so there is no remaining hole
in the earth from it. All of the homes and buildings in
that valley immediately collapsed, and now you can
see where new homes have been built on top of old
foundations. The factories are still a mess of twisted
metal. One of the huge smokestacks is bent in the
middle at about a forty-five degree angle, and the
remains of one of the mission colleges reminds me
of that picture of the Coliseum at Rome. Up on one
of the hillsides is the rubble of a once-famous and
beautiful Catholic church. There is just one door arch
still standing, and all through the wreckage can be seen
the broken bodies of many statues.

As Kazuko and I stood silently in the midst of
this, I tried to imagine what it must have seemed like
to hear the roar of the planes overhead, the blast,
the light, and the crumbling buildings coming down.
As I looked down at the broken stone bodies, I had
an idea of the sensation of seeing real bodies in the
same condition. As I stood there with many emotions
running through me, I suddenly realized that Kazuko
was standing off a little ways, looking in the other
direction. I sensed that there was something real in this

experience for her. I went over and put my hand on her shoulder. Pointing to two walls and a window several hundred feet away, she said, "My father worked in that building, and I am remembering."

Today I read in the English newspaper, "To prepare for war, the United States has enacted a Peacetime Military Conscription. However, one American boy refused to register because of his opposition to war." The article went on to describe the sentence the boy received for refusing to comply with the law. That is a sample of how America looks to many people right now, and it is not giving us a happy feeling.

Sincerely yours,

Marge

Sunday, January 16, 1949

We received a large number of American candy bars that were confiscated from GI's trying to sell them on the black market. We were able to give each girl in the school half of a bar. In the afternoon, one of my students, Tamura-san, came up to me very embarrassed about something. She said, "Don't laugh, but I want to give you something." Then she broke her half of the candy bar in two and gave it to me. "I want to share this with you," she said. This was probably the first chocolate she's seen in years.

And just as a closing fact that I've gleaned from the papers, there are six hundred thousand miles of road in this country; and only 1.1 percent are paved.

Sunday, January 30, 1949

This week I had my first experience at the famous Japanese tea ceremony. In the old feudal days, this ceremony was set up as a restful time for the soldiers and a means of quiet meditation. It is still a cherished institution for the natives (sic), but I think doing the ritual many times would be most strenuous. Perhaps as Westerners we haven't learned the true art of relaxation.

Well, in the usual Japanese way of being ceremonious, we were ushered into this special room that is used only for the tea ceremony. In the middle of it is a small, square hole in the floor for the fire and teapot. For an hour we sat there while tea was served to five people. The ceremony is so complicated that only a few people know it, and everyone else just follows the number-one person, who understands what it is all about. Believe me, after all the bowing, the grunts, and the gymnastics I went through to gulp down a bowl of something that looks like pea-green soup, I certainly began to feel like a monkey.

With this out of the way, supper was served. As you know, fish is not only very common, but the only food outside of potatoes and rice. Well, I have a great distaste for seafood, but I found myself faced with shrimp, lobster, oysters, and a whole fish with eyes, fins, and a head. Somehow my stomach always balks when I see those great big eyes staring up at me, but I have discovered one can learn to do many things thought impossible before.

After the tentative digestion of these delicacies (and by the way, I was saved from eating raw fish), a cage was put over the fire, and we all sat with our feet stretched out to it and under about three blankets. That is the "central heating system" of the Japanese home. At this time the hostess brought the Koto, a Japanese instrument like a banjo except that it is about six feet long, one foot wide and has thirteen strings. On this she played some traditional native (sic) music, which always reminds me of a funeral chant, and yet how out of place it would have seemed had she come out with some American jazz. And that was my evening!

Monday, February 7, 1949

On Friday night about ten p.m., I was called to the door and found several of my college girls in tears. One of the girls in the dormitory was very sick, and in half-hysteria was calling for me . . . so off I went. I've been to see many of the girls when they were sick, but this was my first experience of this kind. The girls who came for me were almost in hysteria themselves; and I realized that if they were lost, no wonder the sick gal was. I tried first of all to get them into a sane state of mind. When I reached Tezuka-san's room (she was, of course, in her bed on the floor), I found six or seven of her friends all around her bed weeping and wailing and talking to her with the light shining straight into her eyes. I could not get them to leave her. Every time I got her quieted down, someone would start talking to her again; so all was lost.

Finally about midnight her family came, but they just stayed in the background and let things go as they were.

I have long ago learned that it is impossible to change some of the ideas of these people, especially in a crisis; so I finally went home, and I guess they wailed most of the night. Early the next morning I went back to see her, and her family then decided to take her home until she was well. It was an education for me, and perhaps I can use it to help point to a better way; but apparently this was a typical Japanese and Buddhist reaction to a situation such as that.

Co-education is being introduced into the school system here for the first time, and it has caused a great deal of discussion. The separation of men and women is a custom that will not be changed quickly. It is only in the past seventy years that girls have had any higher education, and even then it has never been up to the standard of the men. The boys really believe that women do not have equal intelligence. Not only have men always been the dictators and sit in separate sections at meetings, but in some communities even the washing is hung on different lines.

If girls and boys start going to school together from the first grade, then they will learn equally all through the years; but it will never work in this generation because the levels of learning have been so widely different.

This week the girls held their first democratic election, and they were thrilled and scared at the same time. They were electing their YWCA officers, and it was all so strange to them that they were almost afraid to try it. They also had their first discussion group and seemed to make it a success, from the number of people who participated. You have no idea what it means for these gals to branch out into something new: that's something that just isn't done here, especially with women. They realize, though, that they need the practice here in school if they are ever to bring about a new way in the community life to which they will be going soon. It's just like helping a new baby to walk.

Sunday, February 27, 1949

It was the day of the birthday of the YWCA president, and her friends at the dormitory were planning a party for her. I had promised two of the girls that I would help them bake a birthday cake for her; so after class I got my boxed cake mix and frosting, and we went to Okado-san's home. They were all very curious about any sort of cake coming out of a box.

We went into one of the rooms on the second floor and there, in the middle of the floor, did our mixing and stirring. The room is separated from a small porch by a paper sliding door, and out on this porch we built a fire in what seems like a big flowerpot but is really a Japanese stove. On top of this we put the small tin oven—no thermometer, cracks in the seams, and, of course, sitting out in the wind. There was no way of keeping a steady heat or knowing how hot the oven was, and every time we opened the door to inspect the cake we also let in the cold elements.

I couldn't help laughing to myself through the whole experience. How impossible my mother would have thought such a scheme was! But here I was, cooking an American cake in a Japanese manner, and it turned out to be a real success . . . especially for my two friends whom I suppose will never forget how they made and decorated a cake out of a box!

This week I received several bundles of clothes, and I wanted to give some of them to one of the teachers whose husband is sick from the atomic bomb explosion. She is supporting the family of five on her twenty-dollar-a-month salary. Since everyone wears the same dark clothes to school, one is not conscious of the lack of change of dress for another. I knew the family needed help, but I was not prepared for her remark when I gave her the clothes: "The only clothes I have are the ones I have on." She was wearing a pair of slacks and a jacket.

In one of the discussion groups this week, the topic was, "What shall I do after graduation?" Every one of the girls was concerned with spreading the idea of Christian love, which they had come to know at Kwassui. Two girls said they wanted to work in the bank because there was a need there for Christian influence. One of them said her home church was still badly in need of repair, so she was going to spend her time giving English lessons to raise money for it. Nakao-san was concerned because so many of the girls lose their contact with the church when they leave school, so she wants to start a YWCA for young women so that together they may continue their Christian influence and experience. And so the good news is spread. I wonder if we realize how money carelessly dropped into the missionary collection plate really sends the message of Christ into all the corners of the world.

Friday, March 25, 1949

In any country, in any language, there is a certain poignancy in that simple word, "good-bye." We can philosophize all we want to at the time of graduation, but it doesn't detract from the fact that friend must leave friend and all the familiar byways that have grown so dear.

It all started with the candlelight service of the YWCA installing the new officers for the next year. I sat in the rear of the chapel watching the old and new leaders. Six months ago in chapel I saw only row after row of black heads. Now I looked into the faces of friends—girls who in the past weeks had shared with me their hopes and dreams and disappointments. People had become persons. The Japanese music department girls sang in English, "Every Time I Feel the Spirit." The American music teacher sang in Japanese, "My God and I." An international program.

Then came the night and day struggle of the music department seniors to prepare for their final recital, and the English department seniors their graduating English play. When we think of young people in foreign lands, perhaps we are so concerned with their different dress, look, and customs that we forget that their hearts and souls are made of the same stuff as ours. I remembered the final recitals of my college friends, and this was not so different.

At last, the final day arrived. It dawned blue and sunny over the mountains and the bay down below. There appeared on the campus not the same girls that I had known at all. Instead of black slacks and jackets on little girls, here were beautiful young women in their black student kimonos with their family crests on the sleeves, and bright rose or fuchsia silk kimono coats over them. Although Japan is progressing in a new way, she is still steeped in the old traditions of ignoring the individual, rather preferring to respect the hierarchy of authority. So, commencement was not centered on the graduates but on the form and the special officials who were guests. Even though the graduates sat in a special section, it was the officials who marched in and were bowed to. After a hymn, Bible reading, and prayer, the diplomas were granted, not individually, but en masse. The registrar read the list of names, and then the whole class stood up together. One of the girls stepped into the aisle and bowed to the officials. Then the whole class bowed to the president, and the girl received the stack of diplomas for everyone. With another low bow, they were graduated. After several formal speeches by the officials, the senior representative presented to the junior representative the bucket of "living water," symbolic of Kwassui. (The Japanese characters for Kwassui mean "living water.")

After the service, the undergraduates lined both sides of the walk in front of the school and sang, "Till We Meet Again" as the graduates walked out of the building.

And now during the past days, one by one they have come to say farewell before going to the train and home. As I have waved a last good-bye while they walked away with a heavy knapsack on their back and suitcase in hand, I see another life touched by Christianity going out into the darkness.

Monday, April 18, 1949

This is the month that school starts in Japan. Last week the little narrow paths leading up to the primary schools were crowded with little first-year children wearing red ribbons. They all had white pieces of cloth sewed to their garments with their names on them. Each child had on his back his little school bag with lunch, paper, a pencil, and all those little things that every school child needs. The first day when I saw our own little "greenies" march into chapel, I remembered something I had read in my father's diary about his feelings on my first day to go to school. I realized anew the trust that was in my hands in these young lives joining the Kwassui family.

With graduation so fresh in my mind, I couldn't help wondering what these new little girls would be turning into in the next years. I thought of some of my girls who had found the Christian life and had taken baptism before leaving school. Their mental struggles had been the same as mine when I was in college. I pictured also in my mind the recent suicide of another one of our teachers who had been unable to face life squarely. This was the second suicide of a non-Christian teacher in my six months here. What was the possible fate of these youngsters? We have been getting them young when lives are more easily molded. Perhaps we may be able to save them from themselves, with God's help.

During my vacation I went to visit some friends in the only large city on this island. It was a very different Japan, and I thoroughly enjoyed the change. But, the mountains and Bay of Nagasaki, my girls waiting for me at the train station the day of my return, and the red roof of Kwassui on the hill all made the old saying so true, "There's no place like home."

Last Sunday was Easter. It dawned on me very suddenly, for as was true at Christmas, the absence of personal preparation allowed the day to approach very quietly. At 4:30 a.m. our church youth group started out to sing Easter hymns throughout the city and finally ended up on one of the hilltops for our sunrise service. As we sat around on the ground eating our sandwiches after this, I was trying to visualize what the Easter parade at home must be like this year. I've almost forgotten what it must be like to be all dressed up from the hat down to heels, not to mention a corsage. In fact, when I go to the movies, I'm always a bit surprised at first to see that everybody understands everybody else.

This is my week to plan the meals for the Mission House. I think you would have a good laugh if you could look in the window and see me talking to the cook with a dictionary in one hand and gesturing with the other. It is amazing, though, how much of the language I've been able to pick up without any formal study—at least various words to make myself understood.

You must be having a beautiful spring, and we are seeing cherry blossoms. Going to a cherry blossom park is as special to my friends here as family reunions are to us in the U.S. And today, on top of one of the highest mountains here, I found my first violet!

Saturday, May 7, 1949

Japanese life is getting easier . . . and I do mean Japanese life.

We had two holidays this week, so again I turned native. For one holiday I went to Arita, which is the famous "china city"—the place where all the best Japanese china is made—and there spent a day and a night with one of my friends, Tezuka-san. Her father is quite a wealthy man who has had a large cotton trade with America, and the family has lived in the States. We were entertained royally in a house about a block big—a true rarity these days and a change from the hovels of most of the girls.

It was very interesting to see the china shops and the making of the dishes and pottery. Of course, everything is made by hand and painted by hand. Some of the vases and bowls take two days just to have the design put on them. Each piece is baked three different times; and after each baking, new colors are added. The first baking is for twenty-four hours. The second baking is for seventy hours, and then the piece must be cooled for one week before it can be touched. The third baking is for six hours, making a total of one hundred hours each little thing must be baked. Each house has its own mark that it puts on the bottom of each article, and then the person who makes the china puts his name on the bottom.

You may already know that Japanese industry has always been on the family scale. Each family has developed its own trade, which is carried on from generation to generation, and, of course, mostly done by hand. On every street you can look into the open doors and see men sitting on the floor working on something that is his family's trade. They even make their own rope out of the straw left from the rice plants.

The spring colors here are wonderful . . . . First, I noticed that all of the fields were yellow from the mustard plants. Then, everywhere the beautiful white and pink cherry blossoms came up. Now, as you travel you see the fields that are all purple, patch upon patch of this up and down the hills, and all over are the beautiful fuchsia-colored azalea flowers. It just seems there is a pattern—so that as one thing leaves, the other is in bloom universally.

In the meantime, I'm still teaching classes. Right now many of our girls and boys are preparing to take tests to work in the work camps here this summer. There will be three in the country, in which there will be half American youth and half Japanese youth. I am hoping to be in the one near Tokyo where Dr. Kagawa will be one of the leaders.

Thursday, May 12, 1949

When the word *J A P A N* catches your attention, what pictures flash across your mind? Do you think of the cherry trees that turn the hills and lanes into a fairyland of pink and white blossoms? But, can you realize that this event closes the door on days of shivering tiredness, living perpetually in cold, damp buildings with no heat, spending evenings in the home of a Japanese friend where everyone huddles under blankets covering a cage over a fire in a hole in the middle of the room, and seeing students in the classroom with swollen red and blue hands cracked from the cold? Cherry blossoms mean the end of this and that one of the missionaries can take all of our winter clothes to the nearest dry cleaners—a ten-hour round trip standing on a crowded train. In a few weeks, I will make the same journey to bring them back.

Maybe you see the gaily decorated temples with their artistically curved roofs. In the same glance, go with me to my little church where the Sunday school is packed with young children, my Bible class with teenagers, and the church service with young people overflowing the benches and sitting on the floor. Sit in my classroom and hear the college girls speak so naturally of God—more naturally than I could have done. Join the group of boys on my front porch in the early evening hours as they attempt in English to reveal their thoughts and grasp the ideas which I try to share with them. Then spend an evening in my room with some of the seven baptized Christians living in the dormitory of eighty girls, and listen to them describe some of the questions and testing of their faith that come from those who would shake their beliefs. (Though the number of baptized Christians is small, the majority of college girls are studying and seeking.)

Perhaps the letters *J A P A N* give you a picture of ladies in kimonos standing in a beautiful garden in front of a rambling house. There are such things, but there is another view of the country huts made of mud with straw-thatched roofs. Below our house into the rocky side of the hill, people have dug out the stone and put up a wooden front before the hole, making a home. There are the children who are war orphans and live nowhere, and those who have been sold as cheap labor because their families could not support them.

You've heard about the work of the mission schools and you know that a real effort is being made to take Christianity to the people. But, the young people are coming to our churches and schools, and then they return to Buddhist families who have no understanding or sympathy for these new ideas. It is difficult to hold onto these young people in the face of opposition from their families. We must increase our circle of influence and go out into the community—into the homes through social work and health centers.

If Japan means nothing more to you, it at least brings back memories of the war. Also, out in the atom-bombed center of Nagasaki lives a Buddhist priest who became a baptized Christian this last month. He has given New Testaments and been teaching Christian doctrine to his parish of a hundred families. Here we have the need, as well as the contact, to get into the homes through a social welfare center and help create a stable oasis for Christianity in the primary group.

Sunday, May 29, 1949

These past weeks have been exciting ones with two of our teachers leaving for America, the Emperor visiting Nagasaki for the first time so that people can look at him, and the big Catholic celebration marking the establishment of Catholicism in Japan four hundred years ago by Francis Xavier.

Miss Iwasaki will be studying at Scarritt College, and Miss Amenomori will be at the Conservatory of Music in Chicago. Amechan, as we call her, worked with me at my church and has been a grand companion to me since I have been here. The last week as I helped her with her packing each day and we went to so many farewell parties, I couldn't help but remember my own preparations to come to her country, and now she was going to mine. Our youth group had its final meeting for her on one of the mountaintops. The sunset was beautiful; and as I looked from it to my friends around me, I remembered that we were Japanese, American, Chinese, and Korean. There are so many stories of children from different countries playing together, but this was the real thing. I have never felt closer to people than I did then.

We speak of mountaintop experiences in a religious way, but they are so real here. One late afternoon, a friend and I hiked to one of the wooded tops. There, in the grove around a shrine, we watched the sun set behind the mountains on the other side of the bay. Then as darkness descended, we started our return trip. For a while our path led through the woods, and then suddenly we came out onto the fields on the mountainside where the most glorious sight met our eyes. The full moon made the fields a shining silver, and the stars above reaching down to the earth seemed almost to be continued through the lights of the city below and the boats in the harbor. We slowly walked back down into the town, but our hearts soared on high.

The Japanese Emperor is a legend that we are all probably familiar with. Even though the legend has been broken, he is still the beloved symbol of the country. Until the war was over, no one could look upon the face of the man; all heads must bow when he passed by. No one could stay in the top floor of a building when he was near, for then that person would be higher than the Emperor. Many such things have been traditions formed to respect him.

But this month the Emperor is making a tour of the country where his people can see him for the first time. For months, the people of Nagasaki have been repairing, building, and fixing up the city in anticipation of his visit. On the day of his visit, every street in the city was lined with people waving the flag, ready to welcome him. It was not a noisy greeting, but rather one of awesome respect.

Several days later, the city was all stirred up again for the big Xavier celebration. We had spent months training a group of English interpreters. There was even the rumor that Bing Crosby was coming. When the guests finally arrived, they were mostly Spanish-speaking persons! Even the best laid plans of mice and men . . .

I have been overwhelmed by the relief boxes I have received from so many little and big churches that I never even knew existed. I now realize what Christian people can do when they see the necessity. You made it possible for fifty of us to come to Japan last year and for fifty more to go to India next year. You have sent us here; now our hope is that you will help us to do the work that we see is so needed. This can be done by increased giving through the regular channels.

I don't need to remind you of this, but it is something we'd all do well to think about. The U.S. is spending three billion dollars a year on education and fifteen billion dollars a year on war!

The hot, muggy month of July meant a vacation from school. I was free then to participate in one of several first post-war international work camps, which provided me with an unforgettable experience. I wrote about it in the following letters:

Tuesday, July 12, 1949

I am on the train to Tokyo, sitting for thirty-six hours on a straight-back bench in a hot, crowded car eating five *obentos* (like sack lunches) and carrying my own drinking water. Two of my students and I are assigned to join a group of about thirty young Americans and Japanese at a work camp. All of us are paying for this experience. We will spend three weeks working to help build a church youth campground and lead religious meetings in the community. Physical labor consumes about six hours of the day, and the rest of the time will be spent in discussion groups among ourselves and with other young people.

After the work camp, the J-3s will have two weeks of meetings, and then I'll have a week before school starts. That is my summer vacation.

We are just finishing two months of the rainy season—hot, sticky air with rain every day. Every day we are wiping mold off of shoes and books and scratching day and night from ant, flea, and mosquito bites. However, without this hot, damp weather these people could not live, for it is necessary for the growing of rice.

It is a most interesting sight to watch the rice planting. Every inch of land is diked into small areas and waterways that will carry the water to each little field and hold it there. The rice stands in water all the time, and the farmers must work in mud halfway up their legs. It is a curious sight to see them working in the rain with round, pointed hats on their heads and straw matting on their backs as rain protection.

One year of teaching is finished. The successes and failures will become clear in the years to come. I'm certain that missionary life is no different from any other life. The basic problems of people anywhere are essentially the same but just dressed up in different-colored clothes. Perhaps you have the same feeling that many of us did before we joined up—that foreign life is rather queer. It certainly is not. The old saying is so true: "It's all in what you make of it."

I took my college books to the YMCA English class last week; and as the boys looked at the pictures, they mentioned the number of Japanese that were there. I knew that there weren't any in school at that time, so I asked them what they meant. They pointed out to me the pictures of dark-haired girls and boys. I had to laugh about how remarkable this is, for even I think that these Japanese look like ordinary black-haired Americans; while they think that black-haired Americans look Japanese. Surely the first step to unity.

There has been much talk about creating an army in Japan. In one article I read in the *FOR* magazine, the statement was made that maybe we (the U.S.) would have to go to war to force Japan to create an army. That isn't too far from the truth, perhaps, for most of the young people I have talked with are dead-set against the idea of having an army as they are against the Atlantic Pact because of the war implications in both things. Can it be that they have gone ahead of us by seeing that preparations for war can only bring war and not peace?

I wonder if you have been getting reports of the Japanese repatriates who have returned from Siberia as avowed Communists. In fact, that is the only condition upon which the Russians will permit them to return home. I have heard some Americans say that the repatriates should be put into jail immediately, but the

Street Scenes

Carrying things in a *feroshiki*, piece of cloth, rather than in a paper sack

Selling sweet potatoes

A little shop

Babies carried on mothers' backs under warm jackets

Carrying things on shoulder in baskets hung from a pole (passing a small shop)

With My Students

Hike under the cherry trees

Mitsu Takahara, Buddhist (see story of her $9,000 donation to the church in Bartlett, at the bottom of page 141)

Students eating rice balls for lunch in the warm sun

With Dean Hata in front of Kwassui overlooking the bay

Three women helpers at the large missionary residence with male college student who taught me Japanese

Teaching outside in the sun where it is warmer

Teachers' room, sorting care packages

Fond Memories

Students studying in the sun to try to get warm

YWCA Cabinet farewell dinner in my honor

Me with a pick, shoulder-to-shoulder with my students, cleaning up a landslide after a typhoon.

Teaching is more than book learning in a classroom

Bonding with students takes place in the most unusual ways and settings.

English Bible Class

Kwassui teachers dressed up for New Years

Japanese house we lived in

Japanese stove - fanning charcoal fire in clay pot

Heavy *futon* (quilt) over wire crate over charcoal fire to keep legs warm

Our cozy kitchen

Eating at low Japanese table

Our only heat: charcoal fire in *hibachi* (ceramic pot)

Work hard, sleep well

Putting out *futon* (mat for sleeping)

Work camp: making cement foundation
for youth conference center

Larry and I at work camp, moving dirt

Hot Springs heartbreak

Cross and memorial tablet of Christians who died in the hot springs

Hot springs where early Christians were boiled to death
(see middle of page 152)

WALL REMNANT OF URAKAMI CATHEDRAL

Urakami Cathedral was completed in 1913 after more than 30 years of voluntary labor and contributions by Catholic believers, and at the time was the largest church in the Orient.

The sturdy brick structure was devastated by the atomic bomb explosion on August 9, 1945, and the ruins were left unattended until 1958 when the site was finally cleared for construction of a new church building.

This wall is a remnant of the southern portion of the sanctuary which was facing west toward the hypocenter. It was removed to this site at the time of reconstruction. The shifted stone columns are evidence of the tremendous force generated by the atomic bomb explosion.

NAGASAKI CITY

(see pages 152-155)

Nagasaki Park

HYPOCENTER OF THE ATOMIC BOMB EXPLOSION

At 11:02 a.m., August 9,1945 an atomic bomb exploded 500 meters above this spot. The black stone monolith marks the hypocenter.

The fierce blast wind, heat rays reaching several thousand degrees and deadly radiation generated by the explosion crushed, burned and killed everything in sight and reduced this entire area to a barren field of rubble.

About one-third of Nagasaki City was destroyed and 150,000 people killed or injured, and it was said at the time that this area would be devoid of vegetation for 75 years. Now, the hypocenter remains as an international peace park and a symbol of the aspiration for world harmony.

DAMAGE CAUSED BY THE ATOMIC BOMB EXPLOSION

1. Levelled Area: ············· 6.7million square meters
2. Damaged Houses:
   Completely Burned: ········ 11,574
   Completely Destroyed: ······ 1,326
   Badly Damaged: ··········· 5,509
   Total: ············ 18,409
3. Casualties: Killed ··········· 73,884
   Injured ··········· 74,909
   Total: ··········· 148,793

(Large numbers of people have died in the following years from the effects of radioactive poisoning.)

NAGASAKI CITY

Card from Japanese friend
who was in Hiroshima when the A-Bomb was dropped

Across the miles

Seasick all the way
to Japan in 1948

I'm back! In front of Kwassui 1997

50th Reunion
of my students in Kyoto

Japanese people do not seem to be afraid. They all feel that if these returning men are treated with patience, kindness, and understanding, they will soon discover the real truths about the new democratic Japan and discover the error of their indoctrination.

To get away from such profound things, whenever I want to talk about some Japanese festival, I remember the first time someone said to me, "Tell me about your American Christmas Festival." We never stop to think that our special days are as spectacular to foreigners as theirs are to us. In the past months we have had two interesting native (sic) festivals. The Girls' Festival is a time of decorating and exhibiting many different dolls according to Japanese hierarchy. During the time of the Boys' Festival, many huge, gaily colored paper fish are hung on a bamboo pole in front of each house, designating the number and ages of boys in the family. All over the hillsides, the sun reflects from these bright spots that flash in the wind, and the fish wiggle as though they were swimming in the water.

This summer we have had our first fresh vegetables from our own garden where human fertilizer is not used.

For quite a while, I got sick every time we had the fresh things. My stomach was not used to it!

Monday, August 8, 1949

Work camp is finished. This morning I came to Gotemba, the national YMCA conference grounds where one of my friends is at a conference. I've just spent all afternoon sleeping and will have another day of rest before I go to the missionary conference.

We completed the work expected of us, which was to get the cement foundation laid for the two buildings. You know the big cement-mixing machines we have in the U.S.? Can you imagine what it is like to mix the cement by hand? Can you imagine what it is like to level away a hill by pick and shovel with roots, tree stumps, rocks etc.? It was a great experience.

This was the first experience that the Japanese campers had had of a group meeting with Christians from all over the country. They were thrilled with the realization of the fellowship of Christ even among strangers. It was a great thrill to them and an inspiration to us to understand their lives leading up to and since their Christian baptism.

After the work camp was finished, several of us work campers, both Japanese and Americans, took the night train to Tokyo. What happened on that train trip had a profound impact on me, as I described in this letter:

September 10, 1949

It was almost midnight on the eve of my twenty-sixth birthday. We two Americans and four Japanese were crowded onto the platform between the train cars, standing most of the time. We had tried to sit on our suitcases; but at every stop of this local train, peasants with packs and baskets crawled over us to board the train. It soon became easier to stand all the time. Sometimes we sat on the outer steps of the train to let the fresh night air blow away the smells of the car. Yet, there was always the fear that sleep might overcome us and pitch us off the moving train. Night train to Tokyo.

Suddenly, about midnight, we were conscious of a mysterious stir among the natives (sic). Eyes turned in our direction. We felt unseen hands pushing packages under our feet, and more of them appeared stuffed among our own baggage. One of our Japanese friends whispered to me that the police were coming through the train looking for rice that farmers were taking to Tokyo to sell on the black market. Since we were foreigners, our parcels would not be searched; so these illegal packages had become associated with us.

We looked at each other in indecision. We were puzzled about what our action should be. We knew these peasants were breaking the law; but as our Japanese friends reminded us, they had to play the black market to get money to feed themselves and their families. The crisis passed while we were still debating what to do. It was wrong of us to protect them in this way. It was the old story of law opposed to humanity. We chose humanity. All during the rest of the night people were escaping out the back side of the train into the darkness, and at every stop the police rounded up some who had been caught.

It was not an easy night, standing crowded together in a hot, filthy car. It was impossible even to walk around, for every inch of floor space—even in the toilet—was filled with women and children lying asleep in the debris on the floor. Though this new experience gave us food for some serious thought and discussion, we became terribly tired and sleepy as the night wore on. At one stop, the temptation was great when the police told our Japanese friends that the Americans might ride in a special air conditioned compartment some American military officials were vacating. We Americans, of course, refused this special privilege.

This slight sacrifice was rewarded when Pete, one of the Japanese boys who had been with me at the work camp, looked at me with tears in his eyes and said, "You are truly Christian." He knew we could have ridden in the special occupation car with all the comforts of an American train. (Some missionaries choose to accept the privilege of the occupation.) "I'm so glad I came with you," said Pete, "because we share this pain together." I would not call that real suffering, but I recognized that our enduring this experience with him when we could have had something better meant a great deal to him. The fact that we were willing to live in the way that he must and go through the situations that he had to suffer meant more to him probably than a year of Bible classes. This is a sample of why the conviction is growing in me that we will really get hold of these people when we come to them—not as professional teachers and missionaries—but as one with them, willing to live with their standards and serve *with* them, not *for* them.

I realized again that even though we lacked the training to do good teaching or evangelizing, we might still make a great contribution by simply living and sharing with Japanese young people in the ordinary things of life in a way that the older missionaries could not. Perhaps we are mistaken in our feeling that we must teach and preach on the mission field. Perhaps our better service is merely to live at some ordinary job where we can influence others by sharing in the everyday lives of all people.

This summer at work camp the question was asked again and again, "Why did you pay to come and do the lowest kind of physical labor?" We had to use our bodies for work that hand laborers in the States would rebel at: moving dirt and rocks by means of lifting poles on our shoulders, carrying stones up the hill from the river in boxes tied on our backs, mixing cement by our own muscles, and working hours in the hot sun with only a little warm water to drink because it all had to be boiled for the whole camp. Evenings were spent in meetings or community groups, and all day Sunday we were in the churches. One Sunday a group of us went to a home for widows and children— people taken from the street who were so filled with filth and disease that it taxed all of my Christian love to touch them and play with them. All the time, I was wondering if it were possible to keep from contracting their infections. Yet, they are God's children, too.

Can you imagine the thrill of living, working, and preaching side by side with Japanese friends, together defending our beliefs and loyalty to God against those who would tear them down? In many instances our Japanese friends were verbally attacked because of their association with us foreigners and criticized for their ulterior motives in becoming Christians. On other occasions townspeople brought up bad instances that occurred with the U.S. Army and attributed them to Christianity. But our Japanese friends stood right up to defend us first as Christians, despite the fact that we were Americans. How I admired them.

The old man who took care of our tents when we were away at the work site was certainly not very happy with his job, which was evident from his disposition. However, he, too, was curious about why Americans would live and labor with Japanese this way. One day he had to sit inside the tents because of the rain. He picked up a Japanese Bible from the table and started to read it. After that we began to notice a difference in him. He seemed happy and outdid himself in trying to do little things for us. One day he told the director that he had been studying the Bible since then and felt the same change in his heart that we had seen in his actions—all because on a rainy day he discovered the faith that made our lives as he saw them.

And so, after a year here I still bear the same conviction; only now it is so much stronger. We need to share our physical wealth; but more than that, we need to share our lives. We need to flood the world with Christians in every profession and type of work who want to live ordinary lives with the native (sic) people. Our lot in life was not earned by us but given to us as a sacred trust to keep or to share, whichever we choose. We have committed ourselves as missionaries here, and yet we have come as Americans to live as such. It is my dream, a dangerous one perhaps, for us to someday have the nerve to reject the materialistic standard of living that is ours and set ourselves a hundred percent with those we live.

I have just read E. Stanley Jones' book on Gandhi. It is truly a challenge to all of us to dare to live the faith we profess.

Thursday, September 15, 1949

By the time my second year at Kwassui rolled around, my getting adjusted (though that was never completed) began to turn into my desire to make a difference in the life of students and Christians. Perhaps it is more like I wanted them to see themselves and their world through different lenses. I wanted them to move out of their uncertainties into a more active role and witness. I rejoiced as I saw some of my dreams begin to turn into reality.

Wednesday, September 21, 1949

I have just passed my first-year mark in Japan, one of the happiest years now in my memory.

Happiness, however, doesn't mean the absence of disappointments, problems, and frustrations. At a meeting of my YWCA officers the other day, I was trying to get them to plan some programs for the next few months. They loved to talk about collecting money, cleaning their rooms, and going some place; but every time I pushed the issue of constructive programs, there was a dead silence. Finally they admitted that they had no ideas; furthermore, they didn't know what they should plan. They had no idea what the purpose of the group was. Although I have just started as their adviser, I've had a year of that same thing in other groups; but it still hit me pretty hard. These people are so full of a desire to do something and go somewhere, but they have no idea of how or where to go. I'm sure that in three years I can only begin to get a few new ideas talked about with no hope of seeing much really accomplished. Yet, when you realize that for thousands of years the pattern has been of no individual initiative or thought, only following orders handed down from someone else, I guess you shouldn't expect that in so few years you could bring about a revolution. One must only have the patience to feel—maybe not in my time, but in some time.

My one hope is the new organization of my Bible class. I have two sections for beginners in Christianity now, one only in English and one that will be interpreted. In my English group, since I am the teacher and leader, I feel I can set up the program as I feel best. I want to have discussions on the Bible, work projects, and meetings on politics, relationships, and vocations—all of those things we bring into our youth groups in America that are so foreign to the church here. It gets frustrating always being an adviser when you cannot act but only try to suggest, knowing that nothing will happen. But I hope to set this up as an ideal, so maybe some of them will get the idea and carry it over into other groups.

Last year I talked to students about forming a student government, and now I've written a pamphlet on parliamentary procedure and principles of democracy. It has been translated and is now in the officials' hands. Just wonder how long before that dream becomes a reality.

It is so easy to think of putting Christianity and democracy into the lives of Japanese, but not when we realize that both ideas go against the thought and culture patterns of this nation. It will be a long, hard struggle before the smallest dent is made, but at least we have started.

Sunday, October 16, 1949

Just thirteen months ago I hit Japan! Here is a big project for you to work on. As you know, it has taken me a year to get these folks interested in social service work of any sort of interest outside of prayer meetings and church business. However, this fall, they have finally come around to this idea in a big way. They have decided on a project that I think may be a little too big; but their hearts are set on it, and I hate to discourage them when they've found something they really want to do. As you know, the clothes-washing facilities in the homes merely consist of rinsing them by hand with cold water and no soap, and this consumes a great deal of the housewife's time.

The men of the church have decided they want to buy a washing machine and take in washing for women to help relieve them of that. Of course, there will be a charge; and one of the men, a good mechanic who is now with the YMCA, is going to give up his work to run the machine and sort of manage the affair. Then he will make his living by fixing radios on the side. It is impossible to buy things on the installment plan in Japan. Although there are a few washing machines here, the price for them is about the same as for those in America and not nearly so satisfactory. Last week the men came to me and wondered if I could see about getting them an

American machine that they could buy over a period of several years as money came in from the use of it. They have all the plans for building a little house for it where they will dry the clothes, and they are all excited about the project. I think it has possibilities, and they are so excited about the idea that I am anxious to help them. I think it is important that they do pay for the machine, if some U.S. group could put out the money to begin with until the church can pay me.

The problem is, where can we get the best buy for the least amount? As I said before, I think it is good that my church pay for it eventually. I think it is bad for people here to get the idea that they can get anything they want for free. We are anxious to get the machine as soon as possible.

Monday, October 24, 1949

Perhaps it is the beautiful day, but for some reason I feel especially happy and thankful today and wish to share this with you.

The thrill of seeing changes and new ideas take hold can never be matched by the excitement of feeling results after months of slow plodding. I came back to work this fall feeling so very discouraged, as though my first year had been a blank as far as surface showing went. But now, the fruits of those dark months of concern are beginning to blossom, and no joy can match that of mine in these days.

Last year the school officials insisted, against every plea of mine, that I must teach every high school girl together, which meant I taught each class with girls who could speak fluently and those who knew little English only once a week. This year I am teaching fewer girls two hours a week, so I am able to divide my classes according to ability.

Last year I could never get the YWCA to have any definite programs or schedule. This year they have a regular monthly meeting planned several months in advance and have taken on several service projects. One of the projects the girls thought of themselves was putting pretty posters in the washrooms where the walls were in terrible condition. Last year I taught square dancing to the girls; but this year I will teach a few of the YWCA girls, who will then be leaders for the whole group. Last year we had no high school girl in the fall English-speaking contest because no one got prepared in time. This year before summer vacation, girls were selected and their speeches written before school started in September, so they had two months to practice.

Last year I got some of the college girls interested in working on student government. It has taken a year to get the faculty to accept the idea and both the student and faculty committee to accept a constitution. This week the constitution will be taken to the student body for discussion and acceptance, after which will follow a period of training on democratic procedures that follow a pamphlet I've written on how to use parliamentary procedure. One of my friends translated it. Last year three girls were interested in working on it. This year I don't know how many have been contributing to the first steps. I just wish I could give you an adequate picture of the complete lack of every idea involved in democracy. For example, before vacation the constitution committee announced a meeting to discuss student government. Only a few girls came; but because those few were interested in it, the committee considered that the constitution was accepted by all the students.

I, of course, was horrified and mentioned to them that in the constitution it stated that two-thirds of the girls must accept it before it could be put into practice. They merely shrugged their shoulders. I have since discovered that what is on paper means nothing as far as actuality is concerned. A fine way to start a democratic government. But, they are learning.

Another one of my pet projects at school has been trying to get up some interest in vocational guidance. The Japanese idea is to spend life in study for no particular purpose, and I've been trying to hammer the idea of thinking about vocations into every situation that I could. This year, girls are saying they can see the need of doing some work if I can just tell them what job they should do. There are no vocational tests and no job descriptions—nothing in Japan that can give a student any idea about vocational choices. So, now, the students are beginning to ask for help. I see where we must set up some way to help them. I'm hoping we can have a vocational guidance week that will, in some way, start the wheels rolling in the educational office to try some future planning in that field.

My little church has had as much change in it as any group. For a year I've been talking about social action, only to meet against a stone wall. I suppose there are forty members of the church and maybe eighty to a hundred regular comers. All of a sudden so many things have started to happen—due to many sources, I suspect. The young people have an English class for some of the little children in the neighborhood. Some of the older boys and girls have started a baseball team for teenagers on the street. We are playing with them and hoping to play with some of the other boys on other streets. We are also showing filmstrips one night a week for all the children in the neighborhood, and hope to get the adults in eventually. We're also hoping to put in programs that will attract people who would not come to a religious meeting.

My church also is being the distribution center for all of my relief clothes. They are sharing with the members who need it but mostly are distributing outside the church, which makes me so happy. Some of the members who themselves were repatriates and needed things very much refused to take clothes, saying that there were many other families in the city who needed them worse. They have been investigating hospitals and homes that need things and keeping a list.

Now, the church has been organized into three groups to do social work and is in the process of discovering what areas of need in the city they may serve.

And so, life does work in miracles . . . slowly, but surely. And I suppose we must all remember when times seem darkest, that the sun will dawn—sometime.

So many of the J-3s have said that they feel it is important to go back to the States and try to make a concerted effort to awaken Christian people to the need of making a greater united effort to affect government thinking and direct the way to peace. I don't know what your news is like, but the news we receive from America is daily talk of war, war, war. And I want to cry out, "Where are our peacemakers? Is it futile for me to try to interpret to my friends here the possibility of a peaceful world? How can I talk of Christian love and peace when my country—a Christian country—is continually going in the opposite direction when the eyes of the world are upon it?"

And even though sometimes I want to come home and try to stir the Christian voice that I know is there, though perhaps at times dormant, I have chosen to do my work here and realize that I can only do my best where I am.

People often ask me how I was received and treated in Nagasaki so close after the dropping of the atomic bomb. I have to reply that I never had any unpleasant experiences. In reflection on that time, I think Japanese youth and Christians were as anxious as we American youth and Christians were to be "Repairers of the Breach" that World War II had created between our two countries. We J-3s were—I was—the link, the vehicle through which this could happen. I was touched by the desire and dedication of Japanese Christians to be a source of support for those suffering around them and the American Christians who wanted to be partners with them through the outreach of a helping hand.

Although letters such as the following speak particularly of me, in the larger sense they actually affirm the wisdom of the Kyodan in asking the American church to send young Christians to be in the Japanese schools. It affirms the courage of the American church to send young, untested youth into that post-war situation. It was in that face-to-face meeting and living that dynamic change began to take place in the lives of both Japanese and Americans as we joined faith and vision and selves in creating a new vision of life and the world.

January 19, 1950

Dear Marge's Father and Mother,

It is already eleven o'clock, but I shall not be able to sleep until I finish this letter. I write this letter as one of the teachers of Kwassui, as one of the members of Furumachi Church and as Ame's friend to thank you for your sharing your precious daughter with us and your kind thoughtfulness you have shown us in many ways and your heartwarming hospitality you extended to Ame (one of the Kwassui music teachers who had been sent to the States to study music).

First of all I feel I have to say thank you for your sharing your daughter with us. It really is a big sacrifice. I know it demanded courage to send her here to Japan, which was in such a desperate condition. And yet it is so far away from your country across the ocean. Our country is literally situated on the other side of the world. But I feel now that even the wide oceans or any other possible barriers cannot separate our hearts. How wonderful it is to believe in Father God in whom we can be always one, even when the outward world is against us.

Marge is just wonderful. You have no idea how much she is loved here by the teachers and girls and other people. Once I heard the maids of her house say this, "It is not easy to work in the foreigner's house. Their customs and the way of doing are so different from ours. We could not be patient if we did not have Miss Mayer who understands the Japanese hearts and comforts us so kindly." And also one of the teachers came to me and said, "I am very grateful for Miss Mayer and Miss Boyer's being here. I want to express my feeling but I cannot because I cannot speak English."

Secondly, I thank you for your doing in so many ways for the Japanese people. We are receiving so many packages and big amount of money. These presents are precious themselves and they mean lots for I know that behind of these things how much care, how much time, how much thoughtfulness, and how much prayer are done. Please tell all of those who have been so nice to the Japanese that they have done more than they know and their care for us is bringing the revival to us.

This Christmas, we bought the bicycle to our minister with the $30.00 which came through Marge.

One year ago, we had the dream of a new bicycle and the youth group worked hard to buy one but we had too many things to do to buy a bicycle and we were ready to give it up.

I cannot tell you how surprised but happy Rev. Fujimoto was when we sang "Merry Christmas to you" and took the new bicycle to him.

It is now already twelve o'clock. I think I have to close this soon.

This afternoon, when I was finishing my class of the sixth period, Marge peeped into the room. She was so happy that she could not wait for my going back to our office where Marge, Alice, and I room together. She told me that the laundry machine was already on its way to us. I don't know how to thank you. We shall never forget your care. I understand what a trouble it was and how childish we were to ask such a favor as that. But that will help not only the members of our church, but many of housewives who have no private hours. Everything is far beyond your imagination in Japan. Most housewives don't have a sewing machine nor gas range. They have to cut wood to burn when they cook. It is still difficult to get charcoal and other fuel.

Nobody . . . fortunately I have . . . has seen a
washing machine and if we take clothings or sheets to
the laundry we have to pay more than we can. We knew
it was a shame to ask your favor in such a way as that.
I cannot express my feeling well in my poor English.
What I can say now is just thank you and you will see
what we will do. Please tell them that we shall never
forget their generosity. The church has already said the
word for building the house for it and the work. They're
going to cut down a big tree between the church and the
parsonage and build it there and build tiers of line for
drying.

Third, I say thank you for your kindness and
hospitality you extended to Ame. Several days ago she
wrote to me, "I cannot trust anybody in Chicago. And so
when I return to Toledo, I especially feel at home. That
is my home." She has to have friends in Chicago, of
course, but anyway she calls your home "my home." You
may know this. When she was to leave Nagasaki, she
said to me, "There is one sickness which I shall never
suffer from. That is home-sick. Because I don't have a
place called home." When I heard that, I felt sorry for
her. Her parents are dead, her house was burned by the

A-bomb and one of her brothers was killed on that day and she had been living alone in a small room of her friend's house until she left here. In another letter she wrote that you were her mother and father. Now she can be homesick sometimes. I know Ame for a long time because she was one of my eldest sister's classmates though she is my pal now.

Marge is well. She looks always busy, but she is happy. Her desk is beside mine in her office where Marge, Alice, and two Japanese teachers room together. All of us speak English in our office, though the progress of her Japanese is amazing. I wish you could hear Marge speaking Japanese.

Thank you again for everything you have done for us. I will close now.

Yours truly,

Fusako Kitamura

My own letters continue the story of my second year in Nagasaki:

January 15, 1950

Dear Friends:

Forty-six packages in the last fifteen days. As
the school president says, she should not make me
do anything but take care of relief things, which is
really getting to be a full-time job. But, as I said in my
previous letter, it has really put a spark of life into the
church people.

This week some of the girls found three families
living in a cave near our house. There is a small hill near
the waterfront, and in the side of the hill three families
had dug out a hole in which to live. You have to crawl
into the rooms on hands and knees . . . did I say rooms?
We went to visit them, and later the girls took them
food and clothes. We will go back to visit and try to help
them to want to find something better, discover their
own spiritual needs and give them a mental, as well as,
physical lift. Now the girls are all excited about trying to
find other such places where the people need help.

Some of the people here have been getting replies
from the thank you notes they wrote to Americans.
I shall be glad if a definite contact is made directly
between the people here and the groups who have been

so interested in Nagasaki that they are sending boxes. I hope the interest will carry over to the natives (sic) so that people will soon think of sending boxes and help directly to the people—not just because they know a missionary is here.

Just one and a third years left for me here at Kwassui. It makes me begin to think of what I may do so that my going cannot be missed. I feel that too often we missionaries make a place of dependency in the groups where we are working. I am concerned that in these last months the things I've been most concerned about become more deeply rooted into the hearts and lives of those I've been working with so that it may be a part of them and not go with me.

For your many kind remembrances of me in a personal way at Christmas, I am very grateful. I daily seek to be worthy of your many kind thoughts and deeds.

Sometimes I think I must stay here the rest of my life, but when I remember all the wonderful people at home it seems difficult to give that up.

Sincerely yours,

Marge

Our Japanese House

B y the end of our second year in October of 1950, Alice and I were finally able to move into the Japanese house we had so wanted from the first days after our arrival.

Because we had decided to live as closely with the Japanese as possible, thus choosing the crowded Japanese trains over the more luxurious train cars reserved for Americans, we had felt very uncomfortable living in a Western style multi-person missionary residence with servants. The older, experienced missionaries were not in favor of our moving out into the Japanese lifestyle, but they were gracious enough to give us that freedom. Convincing the Methodist Board of Missions was even more difficult.

Fortunately, the arrival of a new missionary had overtaxed the facilities of the missionary residence, so the board—quite reluctantly—agreed to build a small Japanese house for Alice and me. In Japanese style, the floor was *tatami* (woven floor mats) upon which we slept on *futon* (cotton-filled mats), and the outside walls were glass sliding doors. Cooking was over a charcoal fire, except for rice, which was cooked over a small wood fire. We went to the public bath since there was none in the house.

The following letters describe our first days of the new life we so long had awaited:

October 29, 1950

Dear Mom and Dad:

The end of one week in our new house . . . and we are still living, healthy, and happy in spite of all forecasts to the contrary.

We moved last Saturday. This area is packed with kids. Since the house is practically only windows, you can well imagine that from the beginning of the day until the end and for several days afterward, those kids didn't miss a thing we did—their little noses snug against the window pane and changing position from room to room as we did.

On Sunday we got up bright and early to start our first day's work. We had heard so much about the trouble of starting fires to cook that our only concern was to get a fire started. We got two going, put pans of water over them, and soon the water was boiling away. We were so proud and happy and then realized that we'd never made any plans for cooking. We'd only worried about getting the fire started. We were so afraid the fires would go out before we got something cooked.

Monday was the first day to go to school from our new home. Because everyone had said that we would never be on time for early teachers' prayers, we determined to be on time or bust. We got up, got breakfast, put the *futon* (sleeping mats) in the closet, cleaned the whole house (all two rooms), and just as the last bell rang, we came running into the teachers' meeting. We were not disappointed, for just as we had suspected, all the teachers had their eyes screwed on the door to see what we'd do; and when we came in panting, the whole room went up in a roar. We didn't have time to make our lunch, so we planned to run home at noon to open a can. Well, we ran home and pulled down the can, only to find out that we didn't have a can opener. And I wish you could have seen the kids lined up the first morning. I cut wood for the fire, and they were quite amused at my lack of talent.

Well, this week has been fun, but we are well aware that the novelty will wear off. We won't be so happy to spend so much time on housework, but we asked for it. We get up every morning early enough to clean the whole house and cook breakfast and lunch. It takes about an hour and a half. The house is built more on a hill than the other large missionary residence house, and our rooms overlook the bay so that we go to sleep at night with a beautiful view of the bay. We thought we'd be happier getting out of the big foreign house, but now we realize we are living in a big Japanese house. Even though the three rooms are small, we still each have a separate six-mat room and a four-and-a-half mat room for eating meals and entertaining guests. But to the Japanese, this is still extravagant for two people. Well . . .one step at a time.

Love,

Marge

December 1, 1950

Dear Mother and Dad,

The other night a rat came onto my futon (Japanese mat on the floor). I immediately— or faster—got up and called Alice to bring a hatchet. Well, it was the middle of the night, and I didn't tell her that there was a rat; so she wasn't sure what had happened to me that would call for a hatchet. Anyway, she came and for about an hour we chased the thing around (rather, it chased us), and finally it escaped out of the door.

The next morning at school I was supposed to lead chapel: read the Bible, pray, and announce the hymns. There is a schedule of Bible readings in a series, and I had forgotten to look over the reading for that morning because of the rat. Just before chapel, Alice and I were talking about the funny side of the rat episode and laughing so much that I said to her I wasn't in much of a mood to lead chapel. Then, when I stood up to read the Bible, the reading was the 91st Psalm. Upon reading it yourself you will understand my predicament: "You will not fear the terror of the night, or the arrow that flies by day, or the pestilence that stalks in darkness." I just tried to control my laughter;

and even though I didn't burst out laughing, it was obvious from my voice that something was the matter. I just thought I couldn't get through the psalm without splitting my sides.

Love,

Marge

Subsequent events seemed to support my conviction that we could be closer to the Japanese people if we lived Japanese style.

It was the practice at the school to divide the contents of CARE packages appropriately among teachers and students. After we moved into the Japanese house, Alice and I were called to the faculty room along with the Japanese teachers whenever a CARE package arrived. The assumption was that we were as poor as the Japanese, so they wanted to include us in the distribution of food. I was deeply moved by this. Perhaps no other action could have conveyed to me the sense of "oneness" these Japanese teachers felt with Alice and me. My identity, which had been so important to me from the very beginning, seemed to have been partially realized. Some of the "breach" had been repaired. A measure of peace came into my heart.

It is ironic, however, that it took me twenty-four years before I finally realized that I never could completely identify with the

Japanese. I could never really be Japanese. By then I knew it was time for me to be a responsible American, so I needed to head home for the last time.

While reading my 1950 letters, I note a good many references to my concern about war talk. But this concern was even more prevalent in the hearts of the Japanese. Many of them felt as though the atomic bomb had baptized them into being peacemakers for the world. As the only people on earth who had experienced the atomic bomb, they felt uniquely called to challenge the rest of the world to stop using war as a means of settling international disputes.

March 25, 1950

Dear Friends:

Is peace possible? Should Japan have an army? Birth control? Gambling? These are some of the topics my senior girls debated in English. After each debate there was a period of really good discussion among the class with questions and answers requiring some quick thinking for them in English. To me it was a miracle, not only that they did this in English, but especially that they discussed and thought in any language.

There has been talk in the papers of the possibility of Japan having an army of defense. In the above-

mentioned class one day, the students said that, of
course, Japan needs an army because of military
preparations all over the world. One of the other girls
got up and said, "If we think only of ourselves, we
kill other people and that is bad. We must think of
others first." Perhaps this sounds idealistic and not very
realistic. The news of the H-bomb has brought new
cause to fear and misunderstand democracy here.

We Americans, having forced Japan to abandon
the way of militarism, have become the leaders in
preparations for destruction. How can these people
understand why we do it? It gives them so little hope.
From a pacifist's standpoint I was heartened to see in
the *Christian Science Monitor* that United Nations'
people were questioning the fact that any ultimate
good could come from an instrument of evil such as
the H-bomb. The editor's comment was that unless
Americans are willing to try spiritual weapons, we must
have the best possible military weapons. He was at
least admitting that another way does exist. We here
are all praying that as the Christian church has reached
out its arms in relief to the world, it may also be an
influence on our government to seek peace through the
only possible way—through that of a fighting spirit of

love, and not through the false means of weapons of hate and destruction.

I noticed that Truman has said that we must have disarmament; but until we have disarmament, we must all re-arm. What kind of double talk is this? We've been so surprised to hear from recent missionaries about the militarism in the States and the war talk. I can't see how the U.S. can talk about a democracy and then be so undemocratic in Japan. Of course, the military is not democratic, and it certainly is not providing for freedom of thought and speech here.

The radio news said today that the president is considering the use of the A-bomb in Korea. I hope the Americans have risen up in protest. Alice and I sent cablegrams to the President and I sent one to Taft in protest. We are sending our petitions for the Japanese to sign and send to the President. It is not surprising that he is thinking that, for war seems to follow a certain pattern. Although we can anticipate what is going to happen next, we mustn't stop our efforts to somehow bring that circle to a halt.

Love,

Marge

April 4, 1951

Dear Friends:

Within the past month I've had the privilege of meeting four great persons. I had heard the great pacifist, Muriel Lester, before in America, but this time her message was especially important. Japan has the chance of becoming the first pacifist country. Over a three-year period we have developed a little pacifist group here, and her visit was a climax to our experience together.

I had to come to Japan to hear E. Stanley Jones. When I was at home and heard about the evangelistic campaigns of Mr. Jones and other great men and the thousands of people who were converted to Christianity because they signed decision cards after hearing him speak, I was greatly impressed. But, now I see it is not as simple as that. There are two kinds of people who sign cards: those who want to hear more about Christianity (and most people do) and those who want to be baptized. These latter decisions are not made as easily as we are led to believe from reading about the numbers who sign. Previous to this time are months and even years of steady study and preparation

by ministers and other church people. When the report
goes home, we feel the decisions are made at one
hearing of the message; but we fail to give credit to the
untiring work of those who have laid the foundation.

Mosa Powers Nakayama, alumna of Kwassui, Ohio
Wesleyan, and a member of the Japanese Diet, was
recently sent to the United States to confer about
the Japanese repatriation problem. Because she was
a special friend of my mother in college, she has
always taken a special interest in me here; and when
she comes to Nagasaki, she is almost like a second
mother to me. She had spent some time in my home
in the States recently, so I felt particularly close to
home as we visited together last week. You probably
all know that she was elected to the Diet as a result
of her brilliant campaigning for her husband; the
people decided to elect her instead of him. (Note:
Subsequently, Mosa was the first woman ever to
be given a cabinet post in the government, and she
represented Japan in San Francisco at the negotiations
for ending the war between Japan and the U.S.)

Right after the war in 1946 while I was working for
the YWCA, I was a delegate to the National YWCA

Convention held in Atlantic City. At that time, we
were all thrilled by the presence of the first person
out of that terrible hostile land of Japan: Miss Tamaki
Uemura, the president of the Japan YWCA. Last
week I sat in a little Japanese church and heard her
talk about peace. My eyes were filled with tears as I
remembered that first poignant time we had met in the
States. I remembered how we had been tricked into
killing and dying with the Japanese before, and I prayed
that we might not go into another such disaster again.

With the end of my three-year term here at
Kwassui, I am going to try another experiment for
another year or so. Instead of coming home, I am going
to stay here and study and work on my own. I believe
that I can live satisfactorily on a Japanese salary. There
is some advantage in doing that, instead of receiving
a salary from the States that would necessarily place
me at a higher standard of living. There are many
objections by other Americans to this sort of thing, but
now I have an incurable desire to try it and see.

A Japanese friend and I have been asked to go to
a city farther south where there are no foreigners and
work with the church there. I will teach part time in a

government high school for living expenses and spend most of my time studying the language for a year, doing a little youth work in the church. I want to work into youth and young adult ministry after I learn more of the language. We will leave Nagasaki in August to go to Miyazaki and hope and pray that we may be of some service to our Lord there.

My visit with you at home must be postponed a little longer, but I hope that you will continue to remember me in your prayers.

As ever,

Marge

Full-Time Missionary

At the end of my J-3 time of service in 1951, I stayed on in Nagasaki for several months living with Kazuko, whose father was killed by the A-bomb, and her family of seven in one large *tatami* room on the second floor of a small private hospital where Kazuko's mother worked as a cook to support her small children. Kazuko had just graduated with honors in piano from the Kwassui music department. Her missionary piano teacher, Ethel Bost, made arrangements with her own piano teacher in New York to take Kazuko on as a student for further study. Ethel hoped that I would take Kazuko to the States with me and help her get settled in with this American teacher.

After several months of freedom, I abandoned my desire to stay on in Japan on my own and brought Kazuko to the States for a two-year period of study with this famous piano teacher living in Osborne House on 57th Street in New York City. I finally decided to attend Union Theological Seminary and work toward a joint M.A. degree with Columbia University in Christian education to prepare me for my return to Japan.

After obtaining my Master's degree in Christian Education at Columbia University in 1953, the Board of Missions reluctantly—I frankly told the interview committee I would never live in a Western-style large missionary residence—accepted me as a full-time missionary, and I sailed again on a ship to Tokyo. There I rented a room on the second floor of a *tatami* maker's home while I studied five days a week for two years in a Japanese language school learning to read, write, and speak Japanese. We learned eighteen hundred *kanji* (Japanese characters)—enough to read the daily newspaper and carry on life in the Japanese language. I graduated with honors. I wrote my graduation thesis in Japanese on the Japanese concept of *sabishi* (loneliness). For our graduation play in Japanese, Ted Kitchen and I played the characters of the old lady and old man in the famous children's story, *Shita Kiri Tsutsume*.

In 1955 I was assigned by the Kyodan (The United Church of Christ in Japan) to work as a church and community worker with the seven rural churches in Kagoshima Prefecture. But that is another story. I worked in Kagoshima for the next seventeen years. By then I was beginning to feel that I was living my life as a special person, without fulfilling my obligations as a responsible citizen. In

Japan I was treated as a special person because I was a teacher and a foreigner. In the United States on Home Assignment I was treated as a special person because I was a missionary and had interesting stories to tell. Thus, in 1972 I made the decision to return to the United States to take up life again in the country of my birth.

I need to round off the story of my journey and life in Nagasaki with two related events that happened long after I'd left my work and life in Japan.

The first occurred in Bartlett, Illinois, in 1992.

In 1991, I moved as a retired person to Hanover Park, Illinois, near Chicago. A small United Methodist congregation worshipped in a school gym in the next village of Bartlett. The congregation consisted of United Methodists living in a tri-village area who had been together since 1980. In 1978, Fred and Mary Ann Harbecke, retired farmers still living on their farmland near the edge of the village, had given one of their large farms to the Northern Illinois Conference for the building of a United Methodist church. It was the gift of this land that prompted the district superintendent to knock on doors to see if he could find any United Methodists living in the area. He invited those he found to a meeting in the basement of the village hall. He then challenged the twelve people who came to begin a new congregation and work toward building a church on this gift of land.

These twelve United Methodists didn't know how to go about starting a congregation. Satisfied with their activities in the various churches to which they belonged, they weren't even sure they wanted to expend the energy necessary to build a new congregation. Finally, being people of faith, they knew they had to move out and put their faith into action.

In 1980, when this new congregation was formed, the land given for the church building was out in the middle of nowhere. It just seemed too isolated for a church site. The group began meeting in homes, expanding to the local library. A vacant post office building was then purchased and renovated for worship and Sunday school. Finally when I became aware of them, they were meeting in a school gym. After twelve years of work and prayer, they remained unable to attract enough members to grow into a viable congregation.

The gift of land still lay bare. There was one change, however. Many new homes were being built on the once-vacant farmlands in the surrounding area, making the land a desirable place for a church building.

Finally, in 1992, the small group faced the realization that if they wanted to grow into a viable church and be a witness in the community, they needed to erect a church building. They explored various ways in which they might obtain financial support necessary for building the church but realized they could not raise enough money to build.

The decision was made to construct the building by their own labor and volunteer help from other churches. The small post-office building was sold for seed money, and a construction site manager experienced in working with volunteers was hired. The congregation continued worshipping in the local school building.

At this point I joined the church and committed myself to helping with the physical labor of building. We worked in freezing rain, extreme heat and cold, and mud that came up to our ankles. Men and women, young and old, participated in all phases of the construction. After a year of labor, we were almost finished—with the building, that is. We did not have enough money left for classroom doors, carpets, window coverings, or other essentials to pass the village building code inspection that would allow us occupancy. We did not even have any money for a cross on top of the roof.

It was at this discouraging time that my bank called me to say that a nine-thousand dollar deposit had come into my account from Japan. The donor: Mitsu Takahara of Nagasaki, Japan.

Mitsu Takahara was a young widow when I first met her in Japan in Nagasaki in 1948, forty-four years before. Her husband had been killed in the atomic bombing of Nagasaki in August, 1945. She had six young children to raise. She worked as a cook in a small hospital, and the family of seven lived in one room above the hospital kitchen. Two of Takahara-san's daughters were my students at the Kwassui Girls' School. They had been among the group of students who met my train in 1948 when I first arrived in war-torn Nagasaki. I did what little I could to help the Takahara family at that time, and we remained friends over the years.

Takahara-san is a woman with a strong Buddhist faith. During the years I was in Japan, we often spoke together about our different religions. We found many things we could agree upon: the importance of love, of making one's life count for something good in the world, and of the global family to which all peoples of the world belong. The previous Christmas, I had written to her about my labor on the construction of our new church building. In reply, Takahara-san wrote that she was so impressed that we were building the church ourselves that she wanted to participate in the effort. She spoke of how she had always wanted to find some way to express her gratitude for help given to her family after World War II. She was happy finally to find a way of doing this by contributing a "small amount" to the building fund out of her government pension savings. I thought perhaps her gift would be several hundred dollars until my bank informed me that Takahara-san had sent nine thousand dollars.

I was deeply touched by this act of giving, as were all the church members who responded to my news with tears in their eyes. It was more than an enormous gift of money from an ordinary Buddhist widow in Nagasaki, Japan, to a small Christian congregation in Bartlett, Illinois. To me it was, and is, a testament to the power of love over the destruction and death of war, as well as cultural and religious differences.

This gift not only helped us to finish our church, but it also deepened our own faith and conviction that we must strive unceasingly to tear down barriers of separation and fear. We are called to reach across national, cultural, and religious divisions so that we may extend God's love to all the people in our global family. I think it is appropriate that out of the nine-thousand dollar gift of love we were able also to buy a steeple for the church in honor of Mitsu Takahara.

The second event occurred in Kyoto, Japan, in 1997.

In November of that year I went to Japan to visit the places where I had lived. Kwassui students whom I had taught from 1949 to 1951 decided to have an early fifty-year reunion in Kyoto while I was there. Of the forty who gathered from all over the country, I had seen only two of them during those fifty years. Most of them had not even seen each other during that time. It was quite an emotional

time for all of us. These are some of the comments made in letters
I received later:

- It was so nostalgic for me to remember our life
together fifty years ago. We have all grown older, but
I was so happy to experience that we had the same
feelings for each other that we did fifty years ago.

- Mayer Sensei, thank you for sending me your
picture. I could easily recognize you. Looking at
the picture, I can hear your voice. You are the
first person who taught us the real democracy.

- I look back on my good old days in Kwassui. We were
all young. We were enjoyable every day, though we did
not have so much supplies . . . food, good clothes and all
kinds of other things. In those days Japan was poor, but
our hearts were full of richness, happiness. I remember
when I called on you, I ate up a can of almond that you
served. Once you took me to a Chinese restaurant. How
delicious it was. I never forget it. You used to lend me
your collection of poems when you knew I liked poetry.
I thank you for everything you have shown me. I had

been teaching at a junior high school for thirty-five years after I left Kwassui. I've already retired and now I go to an educational center once a week as a counselor. I'm happy to do something useful to the others. I'll continue this work as long as I am alive and in good health. I'm sixty-seven years old.

- It really was the most wonderful moment for not only me but all my friends to have such a friendly, happy reunion with our beloved *sensei* (teacher) after fifty long years. Though we were in the sixties and seventies, we immediately went back to our school days. We were physically in a hard time due to the war but mentally and spiritually enriched and encouraged greatly owing to your inspiring us. Thank you very much for coming back all the way to Japan giving us such a precious opportunity to meet you again. As you always say, I will try to open my heart with my friends in this small institute and enlighten ourselves in order to make a better society.

- Thank you for your coming to Kwassui reunion. It was the biggest Christmas present for us. You had given us faith that lead our lives. And again your speech gave us the new strength that would lead our coming days. We were very happy being with you.

- How happy day it was for me to be with you! While in Kwassui you always cheered me up by your laughter. You always gave me a chance to think how I had to live as a human being. You did the same for me this time again.

- Seeing you again, I remembered you as a young woman coming to such a different culture as Japan. You must have had many difficult and painful times and experiences, but you never showed any of that to us. You were always bright and joyful and constantly gave us encouragement. For that I thank you from the bottom of my heart.

One of the most touching things that happened at the reunion was when Shingo-san, a quite gentle lady, came to me with a pink envelope. She said to me that fifty years ago when she was a student she had come down sick with tuberculosis. At that time there was not good medicine in Japan, and I had gotten medicine for her from the States. She had never forgotten that and wanted to express her appreciation by giving me ten thousand *yen* (about eight hundred dollars) for me to give to someone in the States who needed help. I was deeply moved and thought about the gift that Takahara-san had sent to our church. After fifty years, someone else was still wanting to express appreciation!!! It was difficult to fathom this. I could only accept and carry out her wishes.

I am touched that women came from all over the country to see me. My heart is so moved to know what I meant in their lives. I feel extremely blessed to be able to know that some of what I had wanted to accomplish and mean with my presence in Japan had indeed happened in the hearts of those with whom I lived. Of course I know what they meant in my life. We were young women together seeking to build new lives for ourselves and a new world where boundaries were broken down. We wanted to repair the breach that had been opened between us by war and hatred.

I told them in my speech that because of them, I had spent twenty-four years in Japan instead of the three years for which I had been sent.

Now, as I think back to the challenge to join the Fellowship of Reconstruction for Japan in 1948, I remember the first words of that challenge: *This might be the chance of your lifetime, and it might be such a tragic failure that you would never be able to forget it.* For me, it *was* the chance of my lifetime. More than that, it defined the journey of my life and became the focus through which I understood the meaning of my life to be. I am ever thankful that somehow I had the courage to make that decision.

AFTERWORD
2008

Since I first landed in Nagasaki over sixty years ago, I have learned more about the history of that era and the dropping of atomic bombs on Hiroshima and Nagasaki and the aftermath of these bombings. These reflections come from that later perspective.

I went to Japan seeking peace and reconciliation with people who had been our enemies in World War II. The same concern for peace and reconciliation that took me to Japan later brought me back to the United States.

During my years in Japan, I had many discussions with Japanese friends about the growing nationalism and militarism of the United States. This looked to them very similar to the nationalistic and militaristic spirit they had experienced in their own country before World War II. They saw the danger of America going down the same road their country had taken. My friends encouraged me to return to the States and work out of the same motivation that had brought me to Japan—peace.

Post-war awareness of the destruction and atrocities that the Japanese military had committed against people of other countries during the war turned many Japanese against their own leaders and militarism itself. Japan went so far as to renounce war in its new constitution adopted in 1946. Highly influenced by the American occupational forces, Article 9 of the new constitution states, "Aspiring sincerely to an international peace based on justice and order, the Japanese people forever renounce war as a sovereign right of the nation and the threat or use of force as means of settling international disputes."

Ironically, as the Korean War progressed in the 1950s, America regretted its insistence that Japan renounce war as a means of settling disputes. America now wanted Japan's help in waging the Korean War. Pressure was put on Japan to revise its constitution to eliminate the renunciation of war in Article 9. This pressure was resisted at that time and down through the years. Japan has continued to resist attempts to remove Article 9 from its peace constitution.

The contrast between the way the United States and Japan commemorate what each did to the other in World War II is significant. Remember Pearl Harbor Day memorializes the bombing of the U.S. military base at Pearl Harbor on December 7, 1941, killing twenty-four hundred military personnel. It suggests we won't forget what was done to us, so we will build our military even stronger to prevent this from happening again.

On the other hand, Japan responded to the dropping of atomic bombs on Hiroshima and Nagasaki by building peace parks on the spot where the bombs exploded. The bomb that dropped on Nagasaki killed nearly seventy-five thousand civilians immediately. A similar number of people died days and weeks later from radiation poisoning. Each year, large peace gatherings are held on the anniversary of the bomb droppings. At this time, strong statements for peace are proclaimed. Those who continue to die each year from radiation sickness are remembered.

Japanese people tell me they have a responsibility to work for peace because they are the only ones who have experienced the horrors of the atomic bomb. They feel a deep need to ensure that no other country endures the horror and destructive power of radiation sickness.

Many years after leaving Japan, I read the book, *A Song for Nagasaki*—the life story of Takashi Nagai, a Christian doctor. Dr. Nagai was the dean of radiology at Nagasaki University, which was destroyed by the atomic bomb explosion. He identified "radiation sickness" as the cause of death among the people close to the blast. He ultimately died of radiation sickness himself.

The bomb was dropped on the Christian community of Urakami, a suburb of Nagasaki. The history of that community is significant. In the 1600s, the feudal lords of Japan became fearful of the spread of Christianity because of the Christians' loyalty to Jesus Christ. Christianity was banned, and Japan became a closed country. Christians from all over the country were rounded up and marched to Nagasaki, which was the port through which missionaries had first entered the country to spread the Christian gospel.

Christians who refused to denounce their faith were killed in a variety of ways. Some were crucified on crosses. Some were boiled alive by being thrown into the neighboring hot springs. Some were tied to stakes in the ocean at low tide and subsequently drowned as the tide came in, covering their heads.

Some Christians managed to escape to offshore islands. For the two hundred and fifty years that Japan was a closed country, they secretly passed down their Christian faith through the generations. They are referred to as the hidden Christians.

After Commodore Perry forced Japan to open itself to the world in 1868 and the ban against Christianity was lifted, Christian priests and missionaries once again entered Japan. Upon hearing that the Christian faith was being preached in Nagasaki, some of the hidden Christians came from the islands to the mainland and asked the priests, "Is the God you are talking about the same God we have been worshipping all these years?"

Now free to worship the God of Christianity, the Christians who had been hidden for two hundred and fifty years returned to Nagasaki and created a Christian community in the Urakami suburbs.

In gratitude for this freedom of religion, the community decided to build a cathedral. After thirty years of volunteer labor, this largest cathedral in Asia was completed. The atomic bomb exploded above this cathedral, which was surrounded by the medical university and hospital.

Nagasaki was not the intended target of the second atomic bomb, following the first one dropped on Hiroshima. This atomic bomb was destined for the steel mills in the northern part of Kyushu Island. However, heavy clouds made it impossible to drop the bomb. So the American bomber crew headed for their secondary target— the shipyards in the Bay of Nagasaki in the south. There, too, clouds prevented them from finding their target.

Then, just as the plane was leaving the area there was a break in the clouds. The American crew quickly dropped the bomb, which landed nowhere near the shipyards. Instead, it exploded just above the cathedral built by the Christian community in Nagasaki. Of the 150,000 people who died in the bomb, 8,000 were Urakami Christians. The death toll could have been more, but many people were away from the suburb when the bomb fell.

Several months after the bombing, the priest of the destroyed cathedral planned to gather those members still living for a memorial service for the dead. He called on Dr. Nagai to say a few words at the service. Dr. Nagai agonized over what he could say to "the bandaged, limping, burn-disfigured and demoralized Catholics who gathered beside the shattered cathedral to offer a Requiem Mass for their dead" (p. 187). He searched hard to find some meaning to what had happened to them. Finally, he had his answer: "Is there not a profound relationship between the annihilation of Nagasaki and the end of the war? Was not Nagasaki the chosen victim, the lamb without blemish, slain as a whole burnt offering on an altar of sacrifice, atoning for the sins of all the nations during World War II?" (p. 188).

He continued, "The Christian flock of Nagasaki was true to the faith through three centuries of persecution. During the recent war it prayed ceaselessly for a lasting peace. Here was the one pure lamb that had to be sacrificed as an offering on His altar . . . so that many millions of lives might be saved" (p 189).

I cannot say that I agree with Dr. Nagai's theology. But I am moved at his ability to take the atrocity done to the Japanese that could easily have been the cause of extreme hatred toward Americans and turn it into a positive interpretation.

Dr. Nagai became well-known throughout Japan. I have pondered the possibility that it was his spirit that motivated the Japanese to memorialize the horrible experience of the atomic bomb into a movement for peace and to prevent the nuclear devastation of any other people.

The voice of peace is expressed in a slightly different way by the Protestant Christian church in Japan, the Kyodan. The following statement is read in the churches each August on the anniversary of the end of the war.

CONFESSION OF RESPONSIBILITY
DURING WORLD WAR II
(adopted in 1967)

The church as the 'light of the world' and 'salt of the earth' should not have aligned itself with the war

effort. Love of country should rather have led Christians to exercise a rightful judgment, based on Christian conscience, toward the course our nation pursued. However, in the name of the Kyodan, we issued a statement at home and abroad in which we approved of and supported that war and encouraged prayers for victory.

Indeed, even as our country committed sin, so we too, as a church, fell into the same sin. We neglected to perform our mission as a 'watchman.' Now, with deep pain in our hearts, we confess our sin and ask the Lord for forgiveness of the peoples of all nations, particularly in Asia, and of the churches therein and of our brothers and sisters in Christ throughout the world; as well as the forgiveness of the people in our own country.

Over twenty years have passed since that war ended; and we are fearful that our beloved country, set in today's problem-plagued world, is once again headed in a dangerous direction. At such a moment, we seek God's help and guidance so that the Kyodan may not repeat its errors but rather may rightly carry out its mission in Japan and in the world. Looking toward tomorrow, we hereby make public this resolution.

Through all the years since World War II, Japan and the United States each have been living out of a different image of the presence they want to be in the world. And through all these years at Christmas time, letters from my former Japanese students encourage me to work for peace in the U.S. as they do in Japan. They are still inspired by the life we shared together when we were young.

I try to be faithful to the experience and inspiration I received from them as we sought to "repair the breach." Now, in our older years, we join hearts and hands across the ocean to continue that journey together started so many years ago.

Paul Glynn, *A Song for Nagasaki*, William B. Eerdmans Publishing Company, Grand Rapids, Michigan, 1988.

To Order This Book

Send your name, address, phone number, and e-mail (if applicable),
with $12.00 per book plus $5.00 each S/H to:

Fruitbearer Publishing, LLC

P.O. Box 777

Georgetown, DE 19947

Phone: 302.856.6649

Email: info@fruitbearer.com

Make checks payable to Fruitbearer Publishing

This book is also available online from www.fruitbearer.com
or from any bookstore (ISBN 978-1-886068-37-7)
Toll Free Orders: 1-800-247-6553

BULK DISCOUNT: Fruitbearer books are available at special quantity
discounts for sales promotions, fund-raising, and educational needs.